THE SEARCH FOR THE
BREADALBANE

THE SEARCH FOR THE
BREADALBANE

Joe MacInnis

DAVID & CHARLES
Newton Abbot   London

To all those who made these expeditions possible.

British Library Cataloguing in Publication Data

MacInnes, Joe
  The search for the Breadalbane.—Rev. ed.
  1. Breadalbane (*Ship*)   2. Shipwrecks—
  Northwest Territories—Arctic   3. Underwater
  archaeology—Northwest Territories—Arctic
  Archipelago
  I. Title   II. MacInnes, Joe. Breadalbane
  adventure
  971.9′9   G530.B7235

  ISBN 0-7153-8800-2

This is a revised edition of The Breadalbane Adventure,
originally published in 1982 by CBC Enterprises.

Printed in Great Britain
by Redwood Burn, Trowbridge, Wiltshire
for David & Charles Publishers plc
Brunel House   Newton Abbot   Devon

INTRODUCTION

There are those today who decry the lack of opportunity for adventure in a world of exploding population, the consequent development of once virgin lands, and the transportation and communication networks that put every corner of our globe in instant touch with every other.

To a large extent they are right — when they speak of the surface of our globe. But there are still two great, almost limitless areas, where exploration has only begun — the outer space beyond our atmosphere, and the inner space below our oceans.

There, adventure still is to be had, and there are adventurers eager to assault these hostile environments.

They are our 20th century pioneers, pushing our frontiers into the reaches where our future may lie. Our astronauts have begun the utilization of outer space with the U.S. space shuttle program. Our aquanauts are pushing ever deeper into the oceans probing the vast reaches which some day may be the principal source of our foods, minerals and, perhaps even, domicile.

Along with our future, under the oceans we may also find some clues to our past. Such is the nature of the Breadalbane expedition.

But out of the two should come invaluable experience in tapping the vital resources that well may lie below the forbidding Arctic ice cap.

As this is written, only the preliminary work has been done on that incredible challenge, but already it comprises a fascinating, gripping story of man's daring and ingenuity and his heroic willingness to take personal risk to further man's knowledge.

Walter Cronkite
New York 1982

ACKNOWLEDGEMENTS

Three people have been particularly helpful in the creation of this book — Jennifer Glossop, an old friend, who drew things together during the early stages, Jill Davidson-Schichter, a new friend, who brought the chapters through the home stretch, and Betty Corson, who readied the chapters for the revised edition. To these three and to all the others, my warmest thanks.

The *Breadalbane* expeditions were made possible by cash and non-cash contributions from a variety of sources. There were individual donors, several of whom prefer to remain anonymous. Since the work began the major supporters have been: Benjamin Film Labs, Benthos Inc., Canadian Broadcasting Corporation, Canadian Coast Guard, Can-Dive Services, Dome Petroleum, Donner Foundation Polar Continental Shelf Project, IBM-Canada, Klein Assoc., Mercury Marine, National Film Board, National Geographic Society, Norcen Ltd., Nordair Ltd., North Water Navigation Ltd., Nova - An Alberta Corporation, Petro Canada, Rolex Canada, Royal Canadian Geographic Society, Scott Polar Research Institute, Telefix Canada.

CONTENTS

PROLOGUE

I t was winter. I stood on the ice of the Northwest Passage listening to the low moan of the arctic wind. Beneath me, somewhere, lay a ship. She was the *Breadalbane*, a three-masted British barque that went down, crushed by the polar pack, in the middle of the last century. Protected by the sub-freezing waters she was a time-capsule, a haunting reminder of the golden age of arctic maritime history. I was determined to find her. All that stood between us was an immense and unpredictable obstacle — the ice.

"THERE'S A SHIP OUT THERE, SOMEWHERE."

CHAPTER ONE

A pril, 1975. The high Arctic. The top of the world. Where the summer sun never sets and winter means months of darkness. The dream of nineteenth-century explorers. Home of the Northwest Passage. A huge, white ocean — and I was swimming under it.

Dancing in front of my facemask was water so cold it could kill within minutes, slamming painfully against the skin, crushing out the heartbeat.

A young man swam beside me. He was an Englishman, an officer in Her Majesty's Royal Navy. For most of his twenty-six years he had been testing himself in the sea and the sky, exploring the limits. Now, once again Prince Charles was struggling to conquer a new challenge.

The Prince laboured against the weight of his diving equipment. His air tanks, lead belt and neoprene suit weighed more than 100 kilograms. He moved hesitantly, trying to adjust his buoyancy. His legs finned deeply into the dark waters. Occasionally, when he added too much air to his suit, his head bumped unceremoniously against the ice.

Keeping alive in this forbidding environment was a constant challenge. Fortunately we had some extraordinary equipment. A regulator, which delivered air at ambient pressure to our lungs, allowed us to breathe. Tiny cells of rubber, called neoprene, laced together chemically into the soft fabric of our suits and kept us warm. By pressing on a pair of valves we could expand or contract our suits, holding a catacomb of warm air next to our skin. But if the rubber was torn or punctured, our suits would fill. Weighted by our heavy lead belts we would quickly sink.

The minutes ticked by. Prince Charles, who had dived before but never in arctic waters, continued to adjust his buoyancy. He gradually dropped deeper and deeper into the water. His eyes were narrow, but his breathing began to slow. He was starting to relax.

Underwater, where talking to each other is impossible, a man's eyes and exhaust bubbles are vital indicators of how he feels. Earlier that day before we had suited up for the dive, I had warned His Royal

13

Highness, "You have to be careful not to let cold water slip past your mouthpiece. A spoonful of freezing water striking the back of your throat might cause your larynx to squeeze shut. Your throat muscles will go into spasm. You won't be able to breathe." He had arched an eyebrow and nodded silently.

In the distance a thin shaft of light from the dive hole wavered in the gloom. It was the only way back to the surface. If we lost sight of it, we would be trapped. There would be long minutes of searching, our air would run out, panic would set in and we would become entombed in an infinite prison.

The Prince was looking straight ahead, his eyes steady and unblinking. His legs worked in an easy rhythm. His exhaled air spilled out of his regulator in even clusters.

I began to breathe more easily myself. Few dives had been weighted with so much responsibility. If this young man surfaced with even an eyelash out of place, I, as his custodian, would be wholly responsible.

As if on some silent cue, we moved in closer together and began to swim away from the dive hole.

Suddenly the ocean flared white with the flash of a strobe light. My friend Rick Mason, diver and cameraman, had joined us to photograph the dive.

The three of us turned and swam back towards the shore. Glancing up occasionally, we followed the rolling contours of the ice past the outline of the dive hole. At the top of the crystal tunnel were a few of the faces that awaited our return: photographers, journalists, aides-de-camp, secretaries, the Royal Canadian Mounted Police, all of them wondering if the Prince was safe.

We swam towards shallower water and a long crack in the ice. On the far side hung a glistening icicle two meters long. Prince Charles swam over and reached out a gloved hand. Inside the icicle, just beyond his finger tip, was a cluster of dun-coloured sea creatures. They were amphopods, part of the enormous web of life that inhabited this remote ocean.

I looked at my watch. We had been under the ice for almost thirty minutes. The dive would soon be over. It was the moment I had been waiting for. I plunged downwards. On an earlier dive I had hidden away two items that I now snatched from the sea floor. On top of my head I placed a black bowler hat. Then pushing carefully against the weight of the water, I opened a large black umbrella.

I began to ascend, rising slowly behind the two of them. Seeing me coming, Rick extended his arm and pointed in my direction. The Prince turned, a thin trickle of air leaking from his mouthpiece. Then his eyes opened wide as if he had seen some monstrosity arching out of the water at Loch Ness.

My heart sank. My God, I thought, I've committed an appalling gaffe. But then the Prince's eyes narrowed into mirth lines. Even through the gulf of water between us, I could hear the muted sound of his laughter. Rick, seeing my self-consciousness, was beside himself. The absurdity became infectious. The Prince swam toward me, gracefully plucked up the bowler hat and placed it on his own head.

The dive officially over, he rose, like Mary Poppins, trailing a stream of bubbles, heading toward the square of light that marked the dive hole. He broke the surface with the bowler at a jaunty angle, causing an explosion of hilarity in the dive tent.

* * * * *

Prince Charles was fascinated by the relationship that England, her Kings and Queens, and the Royal Navy had forged with the sea. On this brief tour across the Canadian high Arctic, he wanted to learn as much as possible about English exploration and discovery in Canada's northern islands.

And so the next morning, a small group from the Prince's party took off from Resolute Bay and flew east about one hundred kilometers to Beechey Island, one of the most important historical sites in the Canadian Arctic. During the middle of the last century, when Dickens was writing his novels and Darwin was contemplating the origin of species, dozens of sailing ships had anchored in the small protected bay to the east of the island. They were part of the greatest navy the world had ever seen.

I was looking forward to accompanying the Prince on this trip — it would be an educational experience for both of us. I did not know then, as I looked down from the airplane at the swirling mist below me, that this day would be the beginning of a long, arduous, and utterly fascinating journey through time.

Our aircraft, a Twin Otter loaded with officials from the royal party, bumped through the sky over the southern shore of Cornwallis Island and then across Wellington Channel. The Prince was in a second aircraft twenty minutes behind us.

Suddenly, out of the whiteness, the cliffs of Beechey reared up just beyond the wing tips. Snow-streaked ramparts, two hundred meters high, rose sheer from the sea. We dropped out of the clouds and headed towards a line of empty fuel drums marking a temporary runway. Just before touchdown the plane, seized by a downdraft, swerved to the left. Both engines roaring, the Twin Otter landed heavily on the snow. We taxied for a moment and then the skis clattered to a stop in the lee of the cliffs.

Outside, the polar wind moaned across the barren landscape. As we swung the door open the gale hurled itself into the aircraft. In single file we battled our way to the door and jumped into the knee-deep snow.

Heads down against the wind, we trudged up a steep slope. The footprints ahead of me were big and well-placed, like the man who made them, Stu Hodgson, Commissioner of the Northwest Territories. Bluff and hearty, Stu was the man who managed "the frozen roof of Canada" an enormous area, most of it in the Arctic that covered almost one-third of the nation.

Stu knew and loved the sea. Some years earlier he had been a union leader on the Vancouver docks. Now, one of his greatest passions was arctic maritime history.

At the top of the slope the blurring curtain of snow parted for a moment to reveal a memorial cairn. Leaving Stu for the moment, I laboriously approached the monument and knelt down to read the words carved in a large marble tablet:

To the Memory of

FRANKLIN

CROZIER, FITZJAMES,

and all their gallant brother officers and faithful companions who have suffered and perished in the cause of science and the service of their country.

THIS TABLET

is erected near the spot where they passed their first Arctic winter and whence they issued forth to conquer difficulties or

TO DIE.

I stood up and inhaled the freezing sea-tang, trying to visualize those heroic men from another century. They would have been stoic, hard-nosed sailors, — English, Scots and some Irish. They went to sea as young boys and grew up before the mast to become patient, tenacious and indomitable, as only men trained by the sea can be.

Like the men, the bluff-bowed, tall-masted ships that had carried them to this place and beyond no longer existed.

I tramped back down the slope, propelled by gusts of wind. With the exception of Stu, all the men had gathered on the snow in front of the aircraft. They had just received word that the plane carrying the Prince would not be able to land because of the blustery weather.

I approached Stu who was staring out at the sea, deep in thought. He was obviously reluctant to leave. It was then that he uttered the words which were to change the course of my life. "There's a ship out there somewhere, Joe, lying on the sea floor, buried under all that ice..."

CHAPTER TWO

August, 1975. A few months later I met another man who, in his own quiet way, would steer me toward the shipwreck. We met on a hill overlooking the sea near Resolute Bay. His blue eyes were fixed on a distant island whose cliffs had turned to gold in the late afternoon sun. Pans of broken ice lay scattered across the sea. A rain squall stirred overhead.

"The ships of the first big Franklin search expedition wintered there in 1850," he said, pointing to the island. "Instead of returning to England for the winter, they dropped their anchors out there in the lee of the cliffs and waited for the ice to freeze them in. From about September to August 1851, they were prisoners of the cold. They lived through three months of total darkness and freezing temperatures of fifty below."

Maurice Haycock, now seventy-five years old, had probably seen as much of the Arctic as any man alive. As a young man he had been a geologist, a student of the inner history of the earth. He was superb at his work. He could sense the geological message of sandstones, siltstones and dolomites, with the same ease that other people read a book.

Each summer, as a scientist for the Geological Survey of Canada, he would go into the field to work, eat and sleep under the huge arc of the sky. In 1926 he went north to Baffin Island for a year — a year during which he was infected with a passion for the Arctic which he has never lost. It was then that he first met A.Y. Jackson who years later became his close friend and companion on many northern painting expeditions. Maurice was thirty-five years old when he began to paint. He carried his paints and materials with him wherever he went and he would sit for hours trying to capture the shimmer of sunlight on rocks, snow and water. Since 1950 he has painted more and more in the Arctic and in the Barrenlands north of the treeline. In his quest for recording the Arctic and the changes wrought by the early European explorers he has become an ardent amateur historian of the events which took place during, as he puts it, "the golden age of Arctic exploration."

That night I joined Maurice in his room in Resolute. In spite of the late hour, sunlight shone brightly through the window. My contribution to the evening was a bottle of dark rum. As I poured, I urged Maurice to tell me something about the Victorian phase of Arctic exploration, when the search for the Northwest Passage was at its peak, that period when Resolute Bay and Beechey Island were discovered and named.

"It really started with John Ross's voyage of 1818," he said. "Ross was a tough and practical old Englishman who tried, and failed, to find the passage. With his two little ships, *Alexander* and *Isabella*, he sailed up Davis Strait between Greenland and Baffin Island. He was stopped by the ice. Wisely he decided to follow the whaling fleet up the Greenland shore, around the ice pack to the head of Baffin Bay. Then he turned west."

Maurice set down his glass and stared at the floor before continuing. "Ross was on the brink of a major discovery, finding the eastern entrance to the Northwest Passage, when in the dim and uncertain light, his eyes or his courage failed him. Any man can make a mistake when he is tired or anxious to go home. From where he stood on the deck of his rolling ship the entrance to Lancaster Sound seemed impassable, closed by a range of distant mountains. But what he was looking at was a mirage."

Maurice described how, a year later, the British Admiralty decided to attack the problem of finding the Passage with two expeditions sent out simultaneously. The first went over land across the high Arctic tundra and was commanded by John Franklin, a young naval officer who had fought against Napoleon.

Franklin's life seemed to be dogged by disaster. As a young sailor he survived Copenhagen and Trafalgar, two of the bloodiest sea battles in history. Sailing the Pacific, his ship was wrecked off Australia's Great Barrier Reef and he spent weeks marooned on a coral island. Later, returning to England on an East India Company ship, he narrowly escaped capture by the French. When he reached the Arctic at age thirty-three, calamity was not far behind.

Franklin's first Arctic journey was a catastrophe. Travelling over land by foot and by boat, he made his way from Hudson Bay to Great Slave Lake and then down the Coppermine River to the Arctic Ocean. Months of cold, hard slogging were filled with poor planning, indifference, and impulsive behaviour. On the return trek south, back across the long stretches of rivers, rocks and tundra, the men endured weeks of starvation, injury and cold. They were forced to boil their boots and eat lichen from the rocks. As discipline disappeared and their spirits sank, they quarrelled bitterly.

Finally, they stumbled back into Fort Enterprise, ragged skeletons on shrunken legs, moaning with fatigue and hunger. Somewhere in the whirling whiteness behind them lay the bodies of those who had starved and at least one who had been murdered.

Further north a second expedition was having much greater success. Commanded by William Parry, a young naval officer leading two British ships, *Hecla* and *Griper*, the sailors forced their way into the eastern entrance of the Northwest Passage.

Then they braced their sails and set their course due west. In Parry's snug little cabin at the stern of his ship there were orders from the Admiralty. They stipulated that his course "be regulated chiefly by the position and extent of the ice."

It was. Fortunately, Parry and his men enjoyed one of those benign Arctic summers when the great waters north of the Arctic Circle were essentially free of ice. Due to magnificent seamanship and favourable weather they pushed their wooden ships over eight hundred kilometers to the west, passing in sight of the shores of Devon Island, Beechey Island and Resolute Bay. As winter approached they pulled into the lee of a small bay on the south shore of Melville Island.

The summer's sailing was not without its problems. They were so close to the North Magnetic Pole that their compasses rotated freely and were useless. At times both ships were surrounded by ice and had to be pulled or warped through. To "warp" the ship the men had to scramble over the cap rail and haul heavy rope and an anchor. They set the anchor on a floe ahead of the ship. Slack was taken up by the capstan. Then the men returned to the ship and winched themselves slowly forward, filling the air with profanity.

When one of the vessels was trapped in a narrow lane of ice, the men often clambered overboard and formed a line on either side. With ropes over their shoulders, they towed the ship forward across the ice like barge horses. Like all sailors in the polar regions, they hated the ice.

Parry and his men wintered in the shore-fast ice for eleven months. The ships' topmasts were lowered. Heavy canvas was drawn across the upper decks and large blocks of snow were banked against the hulls. Then, in the darkness and cold, they waited.

Parry's prime concern was morale. A newsletter was published, a theatre built, plays performed and an exercise programme established. By cultivating mustard and cress and enforcing a strict diet, scurvy, the old nemesis, was kept in check. A year later Parry returned home to England, lionized for his efforts, commander of the most successful sailing voyage ever made in the high Arctic.

Both Franklin and Parry returned to try again. This time Parry failed. His ships were battered by the fierce tides and ice-clogged channels that surround the Melville Peninsula. Franklin was better organized for his second overland journey. He and his men rode shallow-draught boats down the shifting currents of the MacKenzie River. When they reached the Arctic Ocean, they divided into two parties to follow the east and west coasts. The work was exhausting. In spite of high winds, shifting sandbars and freezing waves, the expedition added over two thousand kilometers of Arctic coastline to the map of North America. On this trip there were fewer mishaps. Only two men died, one from tuberculosis and the other from drowning.

At this stage the Northwest Passage, while not yet discovered, was at least a problem reduced in scale. Thousands of kilometers of Arctic coastline were surveyed and found to be navigable. The eastern approach to Lancaster Sound and the Passage had been found. It was now known that at its western end there was an impassable barrier of ice. Between these areas of known geography lay hundreds of undiscovered islands, a large blank space on the map.

Slowly the gap closed. There were more overland journeys and trips down rivers. And then came Ross's famous voyage in the *Victory*. Despite his tarnished reputation and the abuse heaped upon him by the Admiralty, Ross, his hair white and his face lined with worry, was determined to make his mark on the northern ocean.

This time he no longer travelled under the auspices of the Royal Navy, but was in command of a privately financed, one-ship expedition. The *Victory* was an old and decrepit paddlewheel steamer. Within her old wooden hull was the first steam engine to be used in the Arctic. It was a mechanical albatross. It heaved and rattled, puffed and belched and was totally ineffective in the ice. The men on board did what all practical seamen would have done. After cursing it for months, they pulled the engine apart and threw it on the beach.

At the end of their first summer, in 1829, Ross and his *Victory* were anchored off the east coast of the Boothia Peninsula. The Boothia Peninsula forms the northernmost tip of the North American continent and lies west off Baffin Island. Ross named it after Felix Booth, a man who had made a fortune selling gin.

Ross spent four winters in the Arctic. Not by choice. The *Victory* and her men were held prisoner by the unrelenting pressures of the ice against the shore. Finally, in the spring of 1832 they abandoned the old ship, which was leaking badly. They retreated north by foot and by boat, up the iron-hard coast to Fury Beach, on the east coast of Somerset Island. Provisions had been brought ashore there when the *Fury* was crushed in the ice in 1825. Ross failed to contact a relief ship and a fourth winter, that of 1832-1833, was spent there. In the summer of 1833 they were rescued in Lancaster Sound by a whaler — the *Isabella* — the same vessel that Ross had commanded on his voyage of 1818.

In the years after Ross's voyage only a small section of the Northwest Passage remained unknown. It was a gap of less than four hundred kilometers. By the spring of 1845 the stage was set for the final attempt, the doomed voyage of Sir John Franklin.

Maurice stopped and looked down at his empty glass. "That's it for tonight, Joe," he said wearily, "I've got to get some sleep."

Before I left, I couldn't help steering the conversation toward a subject that had been tugging at my thoughts for several months: Arctic shipwrecks. I asked Maurice if he knew of any close to Resolute Bay. He paused, searching his memory.

"Yes," he nodded. "An English ship. A barque. Went down in the early 1850s. Near Beechey Island."

* * * * *

Late the next day, Maurice and I landed on Beechey Island in a Twin Otter about two kilometers north of where I had been a few months earlier with Stu.

Maurice was to fly back to Resolute that same evening. I would spend a few days on this rocky outcrop with my son Jeff, my nephew Iain, and a trio of close friends, including Rick Mason. Zipping up our parkas against the gusty winds, Maurice and I walked down toward the bay.

"The bay," he said, pointing to the dark waters, "is called Erebus and Terror, for Franklin's two ships. Out there, just offshore, is where they anchored and wintered over in 1845." He paused. "What men they were, each and every one of them."

We walked back up the slope and stopped in front of four grave markers.

"Three of these men were from Franklin's crew, men who perished during the first winter. The other is a sailor from M'Clure's ship, the *Investigator*. He was on one of the Franklin search parties."

It was in May of 1845 that Franklin and his one hundred and twenty-eight men set forth from London. They were full of optimism, the last of the large British naval expeditions to search for the Northwest Passage. Franklin, by now an old man of fifty-nine, had specific orders from the Admiralty. "Search for a route in the unexplored region near Cape Walker on the south side of Barrow Strait."

Franklin's two ships, *Erebus* and *Terror*, were three-masted barques, their wooden hulls and beams specifically strengthened for work in the polar oceans. A pair of tough little ships, they had recently returned from a successful voyage to the Antarctic. Their decks and holds were crammed with the best equipment for polar exploration, including a small auxiliary steam engine.

The two ships were last seen in July in the ice-rimmed waters off the west coast of Greenland. A pair of whaling ships, the *Enterprise* and the *Prince of Wales*, found them waiting for fair winds to cross Baffin Bay. On July 26, 1845, in good humour and high spirits, some of Franklin's officers visited the whaling ships. It was the last time Franklin's men were seen. The next day, *Erebus* and *Terror* sailed over the horizon and into the western seas.

At this point, the record of what happened to Franklin grows dim. The logbooks, the ships, and all the men on board, have simply disappeared.

It is known that *Erebus* and *Terror* sailed into Lancaster Sound and then north up Wellington Channel. With winter approaching they searched for shelter and selected the small protected bay east of Beechey Island. High cliffs would protect them from the fierce winds.

I gazed out across the ice. Above it, a sliver of moonlight stabbed through the clouds. I could picture *Erebus* and *Terror* easing into the bay on shortened sail, masts and yards etched against the sky, seamen crouched at the bows throwing out sounding lines to check the depths.

In November the sun disappears for three months and the temperature plummets. After a short time both ships would be locked in, their wooden hulls gripped by the ice.

The men inside the ships, eating and sleeping in the chill dampness, would have been optimistic. They had food and supplies for three years. Each ship had a library of twelve hundred volumes containing such currently popular authors as Charles Dickens. Every day was filled with exercise on the ice, reading and study. A theatre was established. A small printing press was set up to produce notices, songs and announcements.

The ships were unbelievably cramped. Each vessel, only about thirty meters in length, held more than sixty men. The decks and holds were piled high with provisions and spares. Even the officers were confined.

In March and April when the temperature slowly increased and the days lengthened, the men divided into teams and began to travel across the snow on foot, hauling sledges.

They were intent on science and exploration. So close to the North Magnetic Pole, great emphasis was placed on magnetic observations. When possible, they gathered specimens and made notes on the animals and rocks, including the geology of the nearby cliffs. Wrapped in heavy woolen coats and flannel boots, the men trudged up and down the coastline, exploring and mapping its features.

Sometime in the middle of the summer of 1846, *Erebus* and *Terror* unfurled their sails and followed the retreating ice out of the bay. They headed west. After locating the headland at Cape Walker, they turned

22

south into Peel Sound. On board the ships there was much excitement; the men sensed that they were within striking distance of their goal — the Northwest Passage.

During the first week of September, *Erebus* and *Terror* emerged from Peel Sound into Franklin Strait and continued south. Then on September 12, northwest of King William Island, the ice closed in. They were beset.

The ice slammed hard against the ships, squeezing the timbers, sometimes lifting them out of the water. The polar pack refused to release its grip. It imprisoned the ships for nineteen months. For almost two years it groaned and pushed against the hulls, keeping them away from the freedom of open water.

Over the long months of darkness, sunlight, and darkness again, the men fought and cursed the ice. They cut holes around the ships to free them from the pressure. Hours were spent in the crow's nest looking for cracks in the polar pack. More hours were spent below decks, praying, exhorting the Almighty to divide the ice and give them safe passage south.

Nothing worked. Slowly, scurvy set in. On June 11, 1847, Sir John Franklin died.

On April 22, 1848, the survivors surrendered both ships to the ice. It was an awesome decision. The ships were their home, their only way back to England and safety. Led by Captain Crozier of the *Terror*, who had taken over after Franklin's death the year before, they struck out for the stoney shores of King William Island.

It was an impossible journey. Their destination, a Hudson's Bay post of Great Slave Lake, lay more than two thousand kilometers away. To reach it they had to cross a barren land of rocks, rivers and tundra.

The men, disabled by hunger and disease, plodded along the frozen coast of King William Island, covering only a few kilometers a day.

I tried to picture them, struggling along the coast, heads down, thin bodies hunched over, dark coats in tatters, flannel-bound feet cut and bleeding. There would have been a long line of them, in twos and threes, some with their arms around each other. It was fiercely cold. Occasionally, when one of them could go no further, he would stagger off to the side and fall to his knees. There would have been gaunt faces, beseeching eyes, an uplifted arm, and footsteps fading on the stones.

The last of the survivors limped across the ice of Simpson Strait, south of King William Island, toward the low drumlin outline of mainland Canada. There were only about thirty left. Their final encampment was on the rocky shore of a place called Starvation Cove. Here they knelt down, huddled in the snow, and breathed their last.

Hours later, long after the Twin Otter had taken Maurice back to Resolute, I stirred from a restless sleep. In the cold night air, fingers of frost had gathered on top of my sleeping bag. Outside the tent, the midnight sun bathed the line of hills around the bay in soft twilight. I dressed quickly, trying not to disturb the others. Slipping outside, I made my way quietly down the slope.

I walked to the shore and dipped my hand into the ocean. It had been almost five years to the day that I had brought my first diving expedition into the high Arctic. In August of 1970, we had camped on the eastern shore of Resolute Bay. There were only four of us then and our goals had been simple: to learn as much as we could about the systems and techniques of Arctic diving; to use what we had learned in the earth's warmer waters — about suits, breathing regulators and other equipment — and apply it to this final ocean frontier, to allow a diver to work under the ice, safely and efficiently.

Since then, I had come back up north at least once each year, the expeditions growing in size and complexity, but the objective remaining the same: to learn how to deal with the ocean and its cover of ice. By 1974, the participants in my expeditions had made over eight hundred dives at twenty-nine different dive sites, including Baffin Island, the north coast of Alaska and the North Pole.

There had been some exceptional highlights: building Sub-Igloo, the world's first manned polar station; the first face-to-face encounters with bowhead and beluga whales; and of course the uncontestable drama of being the first divers to film under the North Pole.

I stood up and looked at the eastern sky. Searching for a shipwreck was an intriguing idea. It would be both a historical odyssey and a chance to extend Arctic underwater technology. But was it worth it? Shipwrecks were a fool's game, the province of the rich and obsessed, especially in these waters, covered with ice and the breath of the Pleistocene. Although I knew a little about the sea, I was not a marine archaeologist. Yet somehow Beechey Island had taken hold of me, compelling me to explore her secrets. I couldn't explain it. I still can't. I just knew I couldn't resist.

On our last day, Rick Mason and I dived beneath the waters of the bay to make a brief reconnaissance of the general area where *Erebus* and *Terror* had dropped their anchors more than a hundred years before. We stood on the shore and strapped ourselves into our gear. Rick moved with practiced rhythms, shifting the weight of his air cylinder along his spine, tightening his shoulder straps, smoothing the neoprene gloves that covered his hands.

I followed him into the sea, moving slowly in the dark swirls created by his body's passage through the water. As we went in deeper, our land-bound awkwardness left us; we became buoyant, lifted by the sea. We ran our eyes over each other's equipment, checking, taking nothing for granted. We began the descent by swimming under a pan of ice. Below us, the sea floor sloped softly away, heavy with silt and an occasional oval depression. I peered over the edge of one of the depressions; it had been made recently by the grinding force of the ice.

We followed the downward curve of the bay and within minutes were several hundred meters off shore.

With Rick in the lead, one hand grasping his underwater camera, we turned and swam parallel to the shore. We were deep now, below ten meters down where the cold ocean compressed our diving suits and pushed hard against our skin.

For twenty-five minutes we saw nothing on the sea floor. I wasn't exactly sure of what we hoped to find, but certainly something more than a few brittle stars and sea urchins.

As we turned in toward shore and started up a low incline, my facemask began to fill with cold water. The more I purged, the faster it filled. I signalled to Rick that I was going up.

Close to the surface the water began to dance against my eyes and sting my nostrils. I decided to stay on top and swim in toward the shallows until I could fix my mask. Cursing the awkwardness of my thick neoprene gloves, I stood chest-high in the water and tried to empty my facemask. As soon as I went underwater, the mask filled again. Fumbling and swearing in the cold and rain, I tried to fix it. Then I thought of Rick. He should have caught up with me. I worked quickly.

Suddenly, a neoprene body surfaced beside me.

"I'm sorry I'm late, but I thought you might be interested in this." Rick lifted a long piece of wood out of the sea. Curved, dark with age, the hand-worked timber held four copper nails. It was old, very old.

Awed, I reached out and touched the timeworn object. What ship was it from? *Erebus*? *Terror*? One of the search expeditions? Perhaps the ship that Maurice had mentioned?

I took the timber from Rick and held it in my hands. Water dripped from the grain of the wood and fell into the ocean. For a fleeting moment there was a rare and marvelous fusion between man, object and sea, a fusion that would sustain me through the challenge of the next five years.

CHAPTER THREE

S eptember, 1975. A few weeks later on my way back from giving a
lecture in Stockholm, I went to England. It was the beginning of a
long inquiry, one that would last several years and is not yet completed. It would take me to London, Greenwich, Cambridge; to the
National Maritime Museum, the Public Records Office, the British
Museum, the Royal Geographic Society and to Lloyds of London. It
was a period of peering along dusty shelves, leafing through old books
and papers and asking questions.

Of all the places I visited in England, none was more compelling
than the Scott Polar Research Institute in Cambridge. Here, in a small
red-bricked building under the shade trees of Lensfield Road, was the
world's finest collection of polar literature. On the ground floor
museum and in the basement archives were the ghosts of Scott, Franklin, Shackelton and other explorers and scientists who had probed the
Arctic and Antarctic.

One day I climbed to the second floor and walked into a small office
just off the main library. The man who inhabited the office had stepped
out for the moment, so I sat down in the chair opposite his desk and
looked around. The desk itself was a warren of stacked journals and
reports. Off to one side, partially buried by a pile of paper, was an old
black typewriter. A faded map of Canada and its northern ocean hung
on one wall. The other walls were lined with books, old and new, first
and second editions, with and without dust jackets, a silent mosaic of
Arctic history. Among them were M'Clure's *Discovery of the Northwest Passage* and *The Last Voyage of Sir John Franklin* by R.J.
Cyriax.

A thick manuscript, heavily edited, was lying on the desk. It bore
an imposing title: *The Exploration of Northern Canada, 500 to 1920, A
Chronology.*

The book began with the Irish voyages of Saint Brendan in the year
500. It ended, almost 600 pages later, with the 1920 expedition of
Donald MacMillan. Inside were over five thousand entries, single

paragraph summaries of men in ships, men on foot, ship voyages and sledge journeys, a compendium of fourteen centuries of human activity on a freezing ocean and the iron-hard islands and peninsulas that divided it. Each page was a painstakingly researched account of human endeavour, a litany of hope and hardship. It was co-authored by the man who worked at this desk, Clive Holland, a man who had never set foot in the Arctic.

Just then he walked in. Easing his slim frame into a chair, Holland ran a hand through his thinning black hair. His face was angular, scholarly, the kind that peers easily into books. Raising an eyebrow skeptically, he leaned across the desk.

"I still can't believe that you'd like to find a sunken ship under all that ice," he said. "No one, as far as I know, has ever gone searching for a drowned ship so far north."

He was right. But then no one had spent so much time under the arctic ice as the divers on my expeditions. In earlier conversations with Clive I had described how hundreds of dives, made beneath shorefast and drifting ice, had built up our confidence and given us a chance to study the use of sophisticated underwater equipment. On one of our projects in 1974, a group of professionals from Vancouver had made a series of dives to seventy-five meters. They had gone down beneath the ice of the Northwest Passage, breathing an exotic mixture of oxygen and helium, demonstrating that even in polar waters it was possible to dive deep and work hard. Today I tried to outline the implications of being able to stay under the Arctic Ocean for long periods of work.

"It gives us access to all those ships that foundered and sank in near-shore waters," I said. "A shipwreck, if we could find one, would provide a splendid opportunity to focus everything we've learned — about diving, cameras, lighting systems. It would mean we could put together a full scientific programme of marine archaeology, biology and sea-ice studies. It would be historically important too. Salvaged items of a ship's cargo, or the crew's personal property, might reveal aspects of life on board that are unavailable from standard sources such as mariners' logs or bills of lading. Such a search would be really exciting. I can't think of a greater challenge."

Clive shook his head slowly and began to leaf through some papers at the side of his desk. He murmured something, barely audible, that sounded like "not bloody likely..."

The conversation struggled forward; the man from the ice-floes talking to the man from the library. It took several hours of conversation, some of it in the deep shadows of a nearby pub, before we reached the bridge that joined us.

A daguerreotype of Sir John Franklin just prior to the departure of his expedition in May of 1845. He was fifty-nine years old and optimistic about finding the Northwest Passage.
© *Scott Polar Research Institute*

A lithograph drawn by Captain Inglefield of the sinking of the Breadalbane *on August 21st, 1853. Captain Inglefield was on HMS* Phoenix.
© *Scott Polar Research Institute*

Doug Elsey, Phil Nuytten and Jeff MacInnis are pictured in one of the Zodiacs, searching for the Breadalbane *in the lee of Beechey Island in 1978. For the moment, the area is free of ice. The* Breadalbane *was later found further off shore.*
© *Undersea Research*

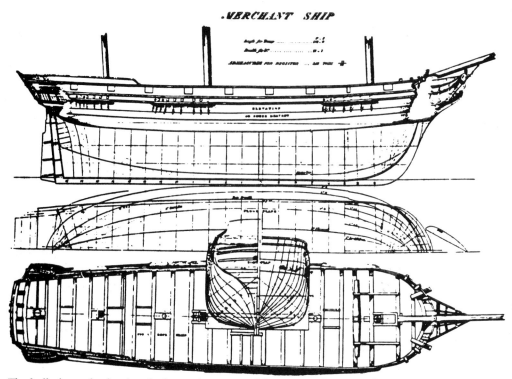

The hull plans of a five-hundred-ton, three-masted barque similar to the Breadalbane.
© *National Maritime Museum*

Photographer Rick Mason filming Beechey Island and the ice in Erebus and Terror Bay during the 1978 expedition.
© Undersea Research

Landing on the smooth, shorefast ice near Beechey Island. The ice over the Breadalbane *is similar to the sheer ridges pictured in the foreground.*
Emory Kristof—©National Geographic Society

A view towards the stern of the Labrador *in 1978 showing the broken and jammed ice which kept fouling the side-scan sonar tow-cable.*
Emory Kristof — © *National Geographic Society*

From the right, Captain Claude Green, Gary Kozak and Joe MacInnis on the bridge of the Labrador *in 1979, discussing the reasons for giving up the search.*
Emory Kristof — ©*National Geographic Society*

Phil Nuytten checks out the search equipment during the 1978 expedition.
©*Undersea Research*

A close-up view of spring sea-ice conditions over the Breadalbane *site in 1981. Similar conditions were found in 1982.*
Emory Kristof — ©National Geographic Society

Underwater partners Joe MacInnis and the Remote Piloted Vehicle (RPV) aboard the Canadian coast guard breaker Pierre Radisson.
Emory Kristof — ©National Geographic Society

"The ship should be close to shore," I said. "Then there's a better chance that the records of her sinking, if any, will be accurate. Especially if there are landmarks in the vicinity."

Clive nodded patiently, waiting for me to go on.

"Ideally, we need a ship in water deep enough for her to be below the ice scour, but shallow enough to be accessible. Something in seventy to one hundred meters would be perfect. Think of it. A ship buried in freezing waters for such a long period of time would be preserved beautifully. It would be like finding a time capsule."

"There are times when I think you must be joking," Clive said. "And then there are other times when I think you are daft. You want to find something less than forty meters long, buried under thousands of square kilometers of ice. In water that is ice-free for only a few weeks each year. Where winds are dangerous and unpredictable and where icebergs weigh up to a million tons."

He shook his head in disbelief and then continued. "There are, however, several remote possibilities. And I stress the word remote. What is needed is an eye-witness account, preferably a log entry made by an officer. It will be difficult, perhaps impossible, and may take a considerable amount of time. But I'll see what I can do."

Months later a brief typewritten note arrived at my home in Toronto. Clive had assembled a short list of sunken ships and approximately where they had gone down. At the top of the list was the vessel that Clive thought had the best chance of being found. She was the *Breadalbane* and she had been crushed by the ice off Beechey Island on August 21, 1853.

* * * * *

She was built in Glasgow in 1843 by the ship-building firm of Hedderwich & Rowan. Her keel was laid on the banks of the Clyde. According to her Certificate of British Registry, issued in 1843, she was a three-masted barque, square-rigged, with a standing bowsprit and one deck. Four hundred and twenty-eight tons burden she was, and from the base of her bowsprit to the sternboard on her mock galleries, approximately one hundred and twenty-five feet long. At her widest point, midships, her beam was twenty-four feet across. Her hold was eighteen feet deep. Beneath her bowsprit was the carved figurehead of a woman.

The *Breadalbane's* original owners were all Scotsmen: Duncan Thompson, a boatmaker; John McNiell, a ship-master; and Daniel MacKenzie, a general merchant. The fourth partner was John Thompson, a wine and spirit merchant.

The *Breadalbane* was a merchant ship, one of hundreds built during the middle of the last century when the age of sail was yielding to the age of steam. She and her sisters carried cargoes of all kinds between the great seaports of Europe: Bordeaux, Nantes, Marseille, London, Bristol, Liverpool, Amsterdam, Copenhagen, Hamburg, Barcelona and Trieste. The *Breadalbane* made many trips south from Glasgow around the Cape of Good Hope and then east and north past the great Indian peninsula up to Calcutta. In March of 1853 she was hired by the British Admiralty to transport provisions and coal to Beechey Island.

The *Breadalbane* left Sheerness, at the mouth of the Thames, on May 19, 1853. On board were twenty-one men including: John Mac-Kenzie, her master; George Bullen, her mate; and George Sabiston, her ice master. The second master was William Fawckner of the Royal Navy. He was a government agent appointed as the Queen's representative on board.

The *Breadalbane* sailed under the orders of Captain Inglefield of HMS *Phoenix*, an eight hundred ton, iron-plated screw sloop which accompanied her on the voyage. The *Breadalbane's* hold was full of coal and crates of food, clothing, rum and other supplies. She was outward bound for Ireland and then across the Atlantic into Lancaster Sound. She was a re-supply vessel, headed for Beechey Island where she would bring provisions to the depot ship, *North Star*. Beechey Island was the main supply base of Captain Edward Belcher's expedition of five ships whose men were criss-crossing the Arctic searching for Franklin.

The *Breadalbane* was born into a world dominated by British ships and sea power. In the sixty years that followed the final defeat of Napoleon, Brittannia ruled the waves. During this time Great Britain was the only truly industrial nation in the world, with preeminence in commerce, transportation, insurance and finance. By the middle of the nineteenth century, when the Industrial Revolution was in full swing, Great Britain was producing two-thirds of the world's coal, one half of its iron and five-sevenths of its steel.

In the early 1840s, Great Britain's international trade was beginning to boom. She possessed a string of islands and bustling settlements that circled the globe, part of the most extensive colonial empire ever seen. An important element that held it together was the sailing ship, thousands of them, part of a magnificent merchant marine that could be found on all seven seas. One of those ships was the *Breadalbane*.

CHAPTER FOUR

O ctober, 1976. After months of deliberation, I decided to take a sabbatical from my consulting practice and move with my family to Cambridge. I had been doing field-work in the Arctic for six years, and now I wanted some time for study, away from the office. Here was a chance to learn more about wider issues — including marine biology, sea-ice, morphology, and, of course, Arctic history. A short bicycle ride from the Scott Polar Institute, we rented an apartment.

Frequently I stopped by Clive Holland's office to talk to him about the *Breadalbane*. As the institute's curator, assistant librarian and author of his own writing projects, Clive was always busy. Yet he somehow found the time to help me with my search.

Sometimes at night when the others had gone for the day, Clive would descend into the archives and leaf through its shelves and boxes. He was searching for a record of that hour, early in the morning of August 21, 1853, when the *Breadalbane* was holed by the ice. He knew two things: the shipwreck site was surrounded by landmark cliffs that could be seen at a distance, even in foul weather; and that officers of Her Majesty's Navy made accurate observations, even under duress. He also knew that the officers kept personal journals in addition to the ship's log.

One day, late in the year, Clive and I went to a pub near the institute. It was one of those downstairs hideaways, warm and friendly, alive with conversation and the soft clatter of dishes. Smoke drifted past the high windows and cold tankards of ale sat within wet rings on every crowded table.

We ordered a pitcher of ale and a sandwich and sat down. Almost absent-mindedly Clive reached across the table and handed me a piece of paper. It was an account of the sinking of the *Breadalbane* written by Commander Inglefield, captain of the HMS *Phoenix*, the *Breadalbane's* consort:

"The ice closing in again obliged us to quit Cape Riley before midnight, and in endeavouring to push the ships into a bight in the land floe, the "Phoenix" touched the ground, but came off again immediately without damage. The whole night was spent in struggling to get the ships into a place of security, but the ice drove both vessels fast to the westward, when, at 3:30 a.m. of the 21st August, the ice closing all around, both vessels were secured to a floe edge; but with steam ready to push the instant the ice would loosen."

"Shortly, however, a rapid run of the outer floe to the westward placed the "Phoenix" in the most perilous position. I ordered the hands to be turned up, not that aught could be done, but to be ready in case of the worst to provide for their safety. The ice, however, easing off, having severely nipped this vessel, passed astern to the "Breadalbane," which ship either received the pressure less favourable, or was less equal to the emergency, for it passed through her starboard bow, and in less than fifteen minutes she sunk in thirty fathoms of water, giving the people barely time to save themselves, and leaving the wreck of the boat only to mark the spot where the ice had closed over her."

The second account was taken from a book by G.S. McDougal: *The Eventful Voyage of HM Discovery Ship Resolute*, which was published in London in 1857:

"On the 20th of August, the wind blowing strong from the southeast, the "Phoenix" and "Breadalbane" were secured to a driving floe about half a mile south of Beechey Island. The ice from the offing closed, and so effectually crushed the transport as to complete her destruction in the short space of fifteen minutes."

I looked up at Clive. He was wearing an inscrutable smile. Here, on one piece of paper, was the information that I needed. I exhaled slowly, light-headed from the ale and the possibilities. I knew I could rely on the information; British officers were known for the accuracy of their observations.

I re-read the most important clues:

Half a mile south of Beechey Island . . .
In thirty fathoms of water . . .

CHAPTER FIVE

O ctober, 1977. For the better part of a year I brooded about the possibilities of mounting an expedition. It would be difficult. To get to Beechey Island, build a shore camp, and run a search more than one thousand kilometers north of the Arctic Circle, would be complex and expensive. It would require substantial financial support and a dedicated team of professionals.

The best charts of the Northwest Passage and Barrow Strait showed Beechey Island to be a mere dot, barely two kilometers across, at the southwest corner of Devon Island. To the north ran Wellington Channel, to the south, Barrow Strait. Gerry Ewing, the former Dominion Hydrographer whom I had once worked for, sent along the most recent hydrographic survey of the waters around Beechey Island. Using this chart it was possible to make a rough reconstruction of the last hours of the ship, tracing her track as she was pushed westward and then crushed by the ice. But what happened after she went down? Did she glide off on an angle? Was she carried along by the currents? Could an iceberg, dragging its enormous weight across the sea floor, have crashed into and moved the ship? Even with Clive's specific information, a search would have to cover a very large area.

Early in 1978, after I had returned to Canada, I drafted a proposal listing the reasons for looking for the *Breadalbane* and several ways we might conduct the search. The proposal, full of technical details, was based on the same premise that guided all my previous Arctic expeditions. There would be very little money; most of the work would have to be done with borrowed equipment and donated time.

In Canada there are a few individuals who are drawn quickly to a challenge. These are men, young in spirit, who ache to try their ambition and experience against something unique. Beechey Island, with its haunting nineteenth-century history, stark, steep-walled cliffs and formidable ice floes, was an unusual offering.

My first choice for the expedition was Phil Nuytten. He was an underwater entrepreneur, the most knowledgeable diver in the country. As president of his own diving company, Can-Dive Services of Vancouver, he had conducted countless searches for objects lost beneath the Pacific and other oceans.

Nuytten is one of those extraordinary characters who, because of his wide range of interests and skills, seems to have emerged from another century. Diver, artist and author, he could carve a Haida totem pole from a piece of cedar with the same ease that he could step into a diving bell and descend to two hundred meters. Confident, outspoken, a born storyteller, he had parlayed his skills and love of the sea into a series of commercial ventures that made him a millionaire by the time he was thirty.

His appearance was deceiving. Nuytten looked like he didn't have a cent. "A character out of the fifties, from the set of West Side Story," is how one of his friends describes him. His long hair is swept back on either side of his head into a ducktail. His nose, broken three times, wanders down his face. Built like a wrestler, he has wide shoulders that radiate strength. He usually dresses in jeans. With the exception of his eyes, a penetrating and luminous blue, there is nothing about Nuytten that hints of his wealth and his knowledge of the ocean.

He launched his first company at the age of fifteen. It was a small dive shop in Vancouver, the first on the west coast of Canada. "It was the days of dry suits that leaked and hard rubber swim fins," he says. "There were no diving schools, only guys who wanted desperately to dive. Some of them killed themselves."

In spite of the difficulties of the new and growing sport, Nuytten's shop prospered. When he could, he spent hours under water. He became a champion spear fisherman, able to hold his breath for several minutes and plunge to forty meters.

In his twenties, Nuytten was a young man in a hurry. There was no time for a formal education. "That would come later," he says, "by reading books." Street smart and sea wise, he rolled his earnings into new ventures including British Columbia's first deep diving company. In 1966 he founded Can-Dive Services and landed his first big off-shore contract with Shell.

About this time, Can-Dive merged with two American diving companies to become Oceaneering International. As an associate of Nuytten tells it, "Within five years they were the biggest diving company in the world, making more money than anyone else, working profit centres from London to Singapore." Everywhere he went, from Norway to New Orleans, Nuytten was respected as a businessman and a working diver, a young man whose brain moved with quicksilver speed. "One of Nuytten's skills is a remarkable intuition," says a friend. "He is deft at all things mechanical from compressors to generators, knowing how they work and how to fix them when they go wrong." So it was with people. Nuytten chose his divers carefully, caring for them, leading them through the risks and tribulations of the business by inspiration and example rather than an iron hand.

In February I talked to Nuytten in his North Vancouver office that overlooked the inner harbour. Outside the window was the busy foreshore and beyond that a parade of large ships, some of them bound for the Orient, steaming towards the First Narrows bridge. Wearing an open shirt, Nuytten sat behind his desk, his feet up on one corner, blowing smoke from a slim cigar. His fingers toyed with a small silver coin he and his divers had found on a wreck in Newfoundland.

"Why can't you look for a ship in the Bahamas?" he said. "It might have some gold on it. If nothing else, we could come away with a suntan."

I mentioned that I'd hoped to set up a small base camp with tents and supplies on Beechey Island. "Keep it small," he cautioned, releasing a perfect smoke ring. "Bring only guys who can contribute a needed skill. No tourists."

Nuytten, who had played a key role in two of my earlier Arctic expeditions, disliked having to deal with inexperienced people who only came to sightsee. They took up valuable space and time. We talked about how we might carry out the search.

"You're the expert," I said, "I'd like you to manage that end of things. You and your people have found sunken objects in far deeper water."

"Let's do it," he said firmly. "Even if we don't find the damn thing, we'll learn a lot about low budget searching under the ice."

"You're right," I agreed. "No matter what happens, we'll learn something. We've got nothing to lose."

THE FIRST
EXPEDITION BEGINS

CHAPTER SIX

A ugust, 1978. We had a problem. It was late in the morning of August 16 and the first phase of the *Breadalbane* search expedition was about to begin. Circling Beechey Island in a Twin Otter, winging past the sheer of the island's cliffs in a freezing drizzle, I could see that the bay to the east of the island was frozen over, covered with ice.

The aircraft, piled to the ceiling with people and packing cases, continued to circle. It would take two more flights to bring all eight people and almost three tonnes of equipment over to the island. The only place to land was on a thin strip of stone beach about two kilometers north of our intended campsite. We planned to ferry our equipment down the shore using our two inflatable Zodiac boats. But today, that would be impossible. The bay was crammed tight with ice. To get to the campsite, we would have to haul everything by hand down the rough and rocky shoreline.

I looked down at Barrow Strait, the wide expanse of ocean to the south of Beechey Island. Somewhere down there, hidden under tonnes of water, was the *Breadalbane*. Overhead floated a clutter of broken floes and pans of ice, remnants from last winter.

I had taken a big risk in coming here this year and knew it. Moving these men and all their equipment, almost four thousand kilometers north of Toronto, had cost thousands of dollars and taken hundreds of hours of effort. I remembered other searches that I had been involved in for objects lost beneath the sea. In 1965 there was the frantic struggle to find the H-bomb that went down off the coast of Spain. A few years later we tried to find the broken pieces of a Pan-Am jet that had crashed off the coast of Venezuela. Each had been found after weeks of arduous searching. At best, with all this ice, we would have only a few days.

Levelling off, the pilot fought the Twin Otter down toward the curving shingle beach. Gusts of wind punched at the wing tips. The big rubber tires skidded on the stones, jerked upward and dropped. We bumped forward to a stop. The first search expedition to find the *Breadalbane* had begun.

The pilot, Dunc Grant, turned a weathered face into the cabin and smiled, "You guys have a mountain of gear. Let's see if we can get you a little closer." Scanning the lumpy terrain in front of the aircraft, he pushed ahead on both throttles. The ancient Otter trembled with the strain. Ten minutes later after crossing shale flat-lands and round-shouldered valleys, he parked on the edge of a terrace overlooking the sea. We stepped down to the flinty ground and began to unload.

We worked feverishly, conscious of the lowering sky. Thanks to Dunc, the campsite was only about a kilometer away. Fortunately there was a narrow lane of water, right next to the shore, that ran almost the entire distance. We inflated one of the Zodiacs and began to move our gear.

I had a large measure of confidence in the men I had brought with me. Senior among the team was Phil Nuytten who strode through the boxes and packing cases wearing a bright orange parka and chewing on his cigar. His technical associate was Doug Elsey, a short, well-built young man with a quick sense of humour. They worked together organizing the search gear.

Doug Elsey was typical of a group of men I call the "sea people." He was a diver and ocean engineer. Born in Thunder Bay, at the head of the Great Lakes, he had always been interested in manned diving and the exquisitely engineered technology that it involved. "Fascinating problem," he said, "human beings going deep into the sea and staying there to work. A real tribute to man's ingenuity." In high school Elsey was not a superb student. However, when he went south to Florida Atlantic University to take a course in ocean engineering, he found his sea-legs. Now he was in Toronto operating Can-Dive Services' office, sometimes steering as many as fifty divers through their underwater paces. Like many men who devote their lives to the sea, Elsey was a blend of romantic idealism and hard-nosed efficiency.

Another member of the team was Rick Mason who had been with me on the dive with Prince Charles at Resolute. Rick was the expedition's photographer and was typical of the many young men who had joined my other underwater projects; extremely competent and willing to work to the point of exhaustion. He had spent years as a television studio cameraman, recording on video tape the dreams and ambitions of others. Yet, in this klieg-light view of the world, something was missing. And then he discovered diving. "It's great to be on this expedition," he said, tapping his finger against the lens of his Arriflex. "Win or lose, success or failure, it all goes into this little black box for posterity."

Working beside him, dressed in a heavy green parka, was Bruce Cowardine the expedition's sound man. Soft-spoken, a cigarette constantly dangling from his lips, Bruce drifted around the groups of working men with his tape recorder capturing the highlights of their conversations.

My son, Jeff, spent much of his time pushing and hauling the gear. Since we had been on the island together three years ago he had become a young man. He was sixteen now, lean and strong, filling out.

Rounding out the team were Bill and Chris Teron, father and son. Bill was one of the financial backers of the expedition who had offered to come north to help out. They moved about the campsite, wool hats pulled tight against the wind, helping to unpack and store the gear. I had known Chris for several years. He was an accomplished SCUBA diver and in love with the sea. His skills at camping and with outboard motors would make him a definite asset.

The final member of the expedition was my black Labrador dog, Moby. Moby had been to the Arctic before. He is great company and his ears and nose are tuned to detect the stealthy footpads of polar bears. At least that's the theory. What actually happens when Moby is released at a campsite is that his nose goes into the air and his body on full alert. His preoccupation is not with polar bears, but on finding the nearest Husky. Preferably female. His ardour in these matters is well known. Once, in Resolute Bay, he took on and defeated two big male Huskies for his love of the moment. Down in the village, when the talk turns to dogs, the people still speak of the sudden appearance, one spring morning, of a mewling litter of "Huskadors."

We had an impressive list of supplies: tents, sleeping bags, Coleman stoves and lanterns, pots and pans, powdered milk, toilet paper, tea, coffee, cereal, cheese, nuts, raisins, over two hundred small packages of freeze-dried food, a pair of Zodiac rubber boats and their 25 h.p. Mercury motors, fuel, including gasoline and naptha for the stoves, a collection of maps, charts and nautical instruments, down parkas and cold water survival suits, two transits for positioning, a Lee Enfield 303 rifle and a twelve-gauge shotgun, a two-meter torpedo-shaped side-scan sonar search unit, seventy-five meters of cable, a recorder, marker buoys, line and anchors, an underwater closed circuit television system with its surface monitor, a first-aid kit, and finally, one case of dark rum and imported French wine.

All of the gear was hauled down the rock slope in front of the aircraft, lifted across a pebble beach and cursed into one of our small rubber boats. Then we took turns pulling the boat along a narrow, twisting ice-choked lane of open water next to the shore. Under the high cliffs at the far end of the island, we emptied the boat and hauled its contents up an incline to a flat stone terrace.

What kept us going during the long hours of building the campsite was the anticipation of what lay offshore — the ship. Each one of the boxes, bags, crates and containers we unloaded took us a step closer to our goal.

Finally, we had a windswept yet liveable campsite. The rubber boats with their new Mercury motors were drawn up above the tide line. A pair of forty-five gallon fuel drums squatted nearby on the rocks. On a raised terrace back from the shore, we built a six-by-four meter longhouse tent. Under its white canvas, we met to cook, eat and discuss the work. In one corner of the tent, space was set aside for Moby to rest between forays.

A smaller tent with dark green walls was put up by the film team. In it they stored their gear and changed their film. This and the larger tent were surrounded by a cluster of small red and orange sleeping tents. These allowed each man to have some time alone. When a group of people are working hard in a remote location, periods of privacy are essential.

On the afternoon of the second day, we climbed two hundred meters to the top of the island for a better view of the ice. It was a hard, steep trek. A foot in the wrong place sent a stream of sharp-edged stones tumbling downward. Fingers and hands were easily cut. Frozen and cracked over thousands of winters, the rocks had a razor's bite.

In single file we made our way up a narrow notch, past sea birds that darted across our path. The only sounds were of deep breathing and the clatter of falling pebbles. The land was lifeless. Nothing grew in these stoney pinnacles exept occasional streaks of lichen, a thin layer of plant life lying flush on the rocks. Far below lay the camp, a collection of toy tents on a narrow shelf between the ice and the cliffs.

It was late in the afternoon when we reached the top and tried to take our bearings. About two kilometers across at its widest point, Beechey Island was a mere thumbprint in the Arctic's vastness. To the northeast, a short distance away; was Devon, the fourth largest island in the Canadian archipelago. Covering thousands of square kilometers, Beechey's neighbour loomed like the spine of a dinosaur, a rambling, snow-swept panorama of cliffs, capes and hills.

Except in its eastern portion, which is totally covered by ice, Devon Island is totally unlike its namesake, that leafy and sunlit corner of western England. Here, there are no green hills, no fields of buttercups, no fragrance of roses. Devon is a gritty, fleshless land of chasms and cliffs. Across the desert of wind-worn stone lies the silence of centuries.

The sea for miles around us was covered with ice. It lay like a vast white plain, criss-crossed with narrow channels that stretched from the base of the cliffs out towards the centre of Barrow Strait.

Our only hope lay with the wind. This corner of the Arctic was known for its severe northerlies. The bay could be swept clear in a matter of hours. However, if the wind continued to blow from the south we might spend the entire expedition locked to the shore. ⟩

We shifted our packs and headed back to the campsite. It began to snow. Large clouds drove in hard across the bay, white on white, a swirling mist shrouding the ice.

That night while we slept, the wind changed direction. It swung into the northeast and then blew out of the north in a series of deep humming gusts. It shook the tent, swirled across the bay, and drove out into the Strait. Somewhere out there, under the long twilight, the great white surface of ice became threaded with lines. Rifts and channels appeared and the pack ice began to shift. Under a wind wild with hoar-frost, the ice began to drift south, miles of compacted rafts and floes, edges jostling edges, filling the air with the sound of bristling crystals.

The next morning I pulled back the flap of my tent and let out a whoop of joy. Everything except the inner bay was clear of ice. With the exception of a few wandering ice pans, the sea over the search area lay clear and open.

We spent most of the morning setting up the side-scan sonar. Under Phil's supervision we took it out of its packing case, carried it down to the shore and placed it in one of the Zodiacs. At the bottom of one of the big wooden cases, Phil had hidden away a diving suit and some SCUBA gear. "Just in case we find it," he said, a big smile curling around his cigar.

Like most inventions, the side-scan sonar was born out of human frustration. Many years ago it was realized that, even in the clearest water, a diver with a face mask can recognize large objects no more than fifty to eighty meters away. However, in most places the sea is murky. In the 1940s, it was discovered that sound — acoustic energy — can reach out hundreds and even thousands of meters into the ocean.

A side-scan sonar is a small, torpedo-shaped electronic device towed slowly just above the sea floor. This device or "tow-fish" as it has become known, emits short pulses of acoustic energy in fan-shaped beams on both sides of the towing boat's path. The return signals, or echoes, are picked up, amplified, and transmitted up a tow-cable to the surface. Here, the echoes are electronically processed and displayed on a graph-paper recorder. What results is a "picture" of the sea floor along an eight-hundred meter path. As the towing boat moves over the ocean, the recording chart displays a wide-area view of the sea floor similar in some ways to an aerial photograph. Under this penetrating electronic window, the bones of the *Breadalbane*, if they existed, would appear as a clearly defined outline.

In the cold, it took several hours to wire up and test the tow-fish, cable and recorder. As Phil and Doug worked, their fingers became stiff and numb. The hours slipped by. Glancing at the sky, it was impossible to tell how much longer the wind and the ice would favour us.

Just before noon, Phil looked up from the side-scan recorder and stuffed a small silver wrench into his pocket. "That's it, Joe," he smiled, "she's tested and ready to go." He casually stepped out of the Zodiac and lit up a cigar. "Keep an eye on the boat for a second while I slip into something more comfortable," he said. His voice was husky, hinting of an old Bourbon Street stripper. Trailing smoke behind him, he ambled up the incline towards his tent.

A few minutes later he waddled back down to the boat looking like a fat Egyptian mummy. He was covered from head to toe in wool socks, heavy boots, wind pants, thick wool hat, gloves and an enormous parka. The inevitable cigar protruded from the fur of his parka hood.

"I've frozen my ass off once too often," he grumbled behind the smoke. "Whatever the loss in personal beauty, old Phil is gonna stay warm."

Doug Elsey came down to the boat equally well bundled up. In his right hand he was carrying an orange life vest. He climbed into the Zodiac, stepped over the mountain of gear in its centre, and sat down heavily. Then he held the life vest up to the sky.

"In water this cold," he intoned, "the only value of this device is to assist in the location of my body."

Doug was right. This was his third trip into the high Arctic. One of the divers who built Sub-Igloo under the ice, and second in command of my Arctic IV expedition, Doug had spent dozens of hours underwater. He knew that, even in August, the Arctic Ocean could kill him within minutes.

I watched as my son Jeff climbed into the boat. Cautiously, he stepped over the big coil of black cable lying on the floorboards and squeezed in beside Doug. A willing helper, he lowered the big Mercury motor into the water, pulled on the choke, and started it with one pull.

The Zodiac eased toward the middle of the bay and turned south. Inside, there was no spare room. The tow-fish and cable were heaped in the centre; the gas tank, a spare, two paddles and a big thermos of hot coffee were crammed in along the sides. A depth sounder and the surface recorder nestled on foam cushions under the bow.

Phil guided the boat using a Canadian Hydrographic Service chart of the bay. On it we had marked out the boundaries of the search area, four square kilometers to the south of the island. Using Clive's eye-witness accounts and the thirty-fathom line, we had selected a zone of highest probability. It lay offshore in the lee of the island's high cliffs.

In a warm ocean, with good weather, a side-scan sonar can survey four square kilometers of shallow water in about a day. But arriving at the mouth of the bay, Phil found a solid sheet and some ragged pans of ice in the central and western sections of the search area. Hidden around the corner from the campsite, the pans were mostly first and second year ice, their fluted sides carved by the constant wash of waves. Since the ice made it impossible to steer the Zodiac in a straight line, Phil had to manoeuvre his craft through a series of "S" curves, leaving large areas of the sea floor unsearched.

Jeff slowed the motor and dropped it into neutral while Doug and Phil lowered the fifty kilogram tow-fish into the water. The cable uncoiled over the grey flank of the Zodiac. According to the depth sounder, the sea floor was fifty meters below. When the tow-fish arrived at forty meters, they stopped releasing the cable and tied it off. Jeff eased the motor into forward and they began to move, steering west. They towed steadily for four hours. Cold and cramped, sometimes ducking under the canvas windscreen for protection, they guided the electronic fish over the bottom. They worked constantly, increasing the speed slightly to lift the tow-fish, slowing it to make it run deeper.

And then they saw the trenches. The first was huge, hundreds of meters long. As wide as a roadway, it wandered across the hidden slope beneath them. Then it disappeared. A few seconds later they saw another. And another. Suddenly, Phil was looking at a seascape pitted with scours and depressions, more like the surface of the moon than the bottom of the sea.

His heart sank. He knew that the scours had been made by icebergs or pressure ridges dragging hard white spurs through the sediments. What appalled him was their depth. The scours were in more than sixty meters of water. If an iceberg had cut into the sea floor at this depth, it must have been enormous and weighed hundreds of thousands of tonnes. It would have been a monolith, a huge white island of incalculable mass and momentum. Pushed by winds and current, it would have been an unstoppable plough, grinding through the sediments.

Struck by such enormous force, a wooden ship sitting on the sea floor, would disintegrate. Its timbers would be torn apart and, within seconds, splintered like matchwood, reduced to a tangle of smashed decks and rigging. Spars, cargo and bulwarks would be strewn across the sea floor.

Huddled against the bitter wind in their small grey boat, Phil and his team continued the search. Far below them the sea floor rolled away, its ravaged surface becoming smoother as they moved out into deeper water. Overhead the sun shifted slowly westward and then slunk behind a bank of high clouds. There seemed to be fewer ice pans now, most of them clustered against Beechey's dark cliffs.

53

As they worked the deeper depths, the side-scan recorder revealed nothing but barren sea floor. The hours ticked by. As the Zodiac completed a turn near the eastern rim of the island, the side-scan made contact with something suspicious on the sea floor, twenty-one fathoms below. Shadowed and black, its outline was different from anything they had seen.

They passed over it again and again, struggling for a better view. The sighting had a quality that immediately arrested their attention. Etched on the graph paper was the hint of something made by man.

"That's it!"

"No way."

"It's a piece of something — maybe the bow-sprit."

"We've got it, we've got it!"

Phil broke in. "Wait a minute. It might be a section of a ship broken away from the hull. It might be a deep scour made by the ice. Don't get your hopes up."

Phil looked across the small boat at Doug and Jeff who reluctantly nodded agreement. All three of them were shivering. They had been at sea for four and a half hours. It was time to head back in. Jeff turned the Zodiac and headed towards land. They worked their way in past the shore ice, clutching the evidence, vowing to return.

That night we uncorked some bottles of wine in cautious celebration.

Later, I slept fitfully. I kept visualizing the *Breadalbane* in all its nineteenth century splendor, masts upright, sails unfurled and then the image dissolved into a huge trench cutting deep into the ocean floor. Half awake, I worked my way into the warmth of my sleeping bag. For a while, I listened to the sound of the wind. From somewhere near the top of the cliffs came the reedy voice of a raven...

...She was moored by thick ropes to a quay in a pool at the edge of the river. A broken plank drifted in and bumped lazily against her sternpost. Her furled sails and long black hull were reflected in the still black waters.

Behind the granite quay and the salt house that squatted next to it, the air was filled with the sound of voices and wheels rolling over cobblestone. Suddenly, a capstan shrieked and someone stepped forward to pour a few drops of oil into the space between the reluctant wheels.

Dockers, stripped to the waist, sweating porters and shirt-sleeved agents moved up and down the quay. A young man in grey canvas trousers climbed the ship's rigging to the highest yard on the foremast. Barefoot and sweating, he worked his way down the yard, his calloused fingers curled around the rope. His feet sought the swaying comfort of the hemp line that arched out from the mast. He did not look down.

From two horse-drawn carts, men with grimy faces and hands shovelled hundreds of lumps of black coal into waiting baskets. The burly porters staggered under the weight, adjusted the load on their shoulders and trudged up the plank to the main deck. They dumped their heavy loads into the hold, swore, then shuffled back down to the quay for more. They had been working since dawn. One of the men, his sooty face glistening with sweat, fell out of the line and dropped to his knees. A small wooden cart with a barrel of water between its wheels drew up to his side. He drank gratefully. Standing, he put his hand on his side and coughed twice. As the man slowly marched off with his fellows, he paused to cough once more. Stepping out of the moving line, he leaned over to spit blood and black phlegm on the cobble-stones.

A gritty layer of clouds drifted slowly toward the ship over the city's factories and tenements. Far below, hundreds of men continued to labour, wiping the sweat from their eyes.

Some time later, a company of sailors made their way lazily up a narrow flagstone street toward the dockyard. They moved in twos and threes, swearing and laughing, their voices echoing loudly off the buildings.

Feeling the warm sun on his back, one of the sailors began to sing. Other voices joined him.

"So haul boys, your mainbrace and ease away your lee,
Hoist jib and topsails, lads,
And' let the ship go free,
Hurrah, boys, hurrah; we'll sing this jubilee,
You can keep the Navy, boys, a merchant ship's for me."

They staggered through an archway into the quiet of the yard. Two policemen looked them over, smiled, and turned away. The men fell silent as they approached the ship and took careful measure of her masts and rigging.

The sailors stopped at a pile of sea chests stacked at the bottom of the ship's ladder. They clustered together, talking quietly, as if trying to lengthen their last minutes on land. One of them, a seasoned drunkard, wiped his flaming nose with a handkerchief. Another scuffed his boot across the cobblestones, feeling the strength of the granite. A third knelt down and picked up a stray dog that had wandered into their midst. Gently he ran his big, salt-cut hand over the brown fur. From somewhere, a church bell struck the hour. Above the men the first mate peered over the bulwarks.

"You down there!" he shouted. "If you've signed for this ship, come aboard and stow your gear. Make haste. There's work to be done!"

Gathering up their chests and bags, the men climbed the ladder. The ship was dirty and in disarray. Like the sailors coming on board, she had become soiled during her contact with the land. For days the dust of the city had drifted down on the spare sails and canvas. In the process of loading, barrels, chests, sacks and boxes had been left along the entire length of the deck. Extra spars lay between piles of timber and cordage. The sailors wove their way through the chaos and stepped into the gloom of their quarters. They had no sooner adjusted to the dim light and tossed their bedding into their cramped cots when the bo'sun's whistle blew.

"Quickly now. There's cargo to haul before we lose the sun."

Divided into four groups, the men worked stowing the last of the cargo. At first they moved sluggishly, stumbling over each other, labouring with muddled heads and the stale aftertaste of ale. The ladders were full with stooped and sweaty bodies working under the constant glare of the first mate and the incessant bark of the bo'sun.

Slowly, cleared spaces began to appear on deck as lumber, barrels and chests disappeared into the hold.

Down below, lanterns had been lit and bare-chested men struggled to fill every cranny with the Arctic cargo: beef, tea, sugar, dried beans and peas, biscuits. Driven by curiosity, the men pried into sacks and sniffed at the top of barrels. Those who could read looked with interest at the signs and letters. Finally they were done. Exhausted, they crept toward the forward part of the ship, took a long draught from the water scuttle and made for the fo'c'sle. Without pausing to take off their clothes, they heaved themselves into their berths. Over their heads a single coal oil lamp burned. Within minutes, the room was filled with snoring.

Outside, a soft breeze blew in from the west. An older man, George Sabiston, made his way slowly along the deck to the bow of the ship. He scowled behind his white whiskers and released a thick cloud of smoke from his pipe. Sensing his approach, a large rat ran out from behind a bollard and scuttled over the edge of the quay.

Sabiston stared at the ship's hull just above the waterline. His old eyes narrowed as if trying to see beneath the planking. Were her timbers thick enough? In his mind's eye, he saw a layer of ice, a fathom thick, pushing hard against her hull. Sabiston stepped forward and looked into the water below the figure-head. Her hull was not protected against ice. He shook his head and stepped back again. If the polar pack put real pressure on her, she would lose.

Just then a boy about twelve years of age walked timidly up to the older man. "Pardon sir, but would this be the ship *Breadalbane*?"

Sabiston looked down at the boy and nodded. "Indeed my lad, this is she. Bound for the frozen ocean." He took one last look at the lines of her hull, then turned away and walked up the plank. The boy, dressed in orphan's clothes and carrying a bag as big as himself, followed at a respectful distance.

In the early morning, the old river gleamed with scattered lights, red, green and white, moving stealthily past each other. A pale haze crept along the shore. Black barges, their pointed canvas sails silhouetted against the sky, moved quietly in the eerie light.

The sailors arose before dawn. Roused by the apprentice-lad, they stirred in their bunks, trying to shake off headaches and thirst. Pale faces looked fleetingly across the room and fell backwards. The seasoned drunkard reached beneath his pillow for his flask and took a furtive sip.

In his small cabin in the stern of the ship, a young man began to write. He sat beside a low-burning candle, his face in shadow, his eyes blinking with fatigue. As the official government agent, Master James Fawckner had been ordered to keep a detailed record of all the stores and provisions brought on board the ship. Methodically, his pen scratched out a description of the cargo, including the number of pounds of tea, hogsheads of rum, and the board feet of cut lumber. His pen slowed and he thought of his woman. He could still feel the warmth of her flesh against his. His pen came to a stop. It would be months, perhaps a year, before they would touch each other again.

As the first streaks of sun reflected across the water, a black steam tug turned in from the river. Some of the sailors paused to look at the bulky shape coming toward them. A tow line was thrown over from the tug. At the bow and stern, rough hands reached down for the ropes that secured them to the dock. They plucked the loops of hemp damp from the dew from the bollards and released the ship.

The *Breadalbane* drifted away from the land...

Early the next morning, I crawled from my sleeping bag, dressed quickly and stepped out of the tent. There was a slight breeze and the sky was partly overcast. Thin bands of light shone down on the hills and headlands that surrounded the bay.

The camp was wide awake. Doug and Phil were down at the shore, preparing the Zodiac for its morning run. From inside the longhouse tent I heard muffled voices, the sound of men gathering around the cookstove for breakfast.

A meal on a high Arctic shore is, quite simply, water added to everything. It is poured over tea leaves, mixed with porridge and stirred in with freeze-dried scrambled eggs. Meals are hardly a gourmet's delight.

After a morning meeting to talk over the day's plans, we moved outside the longhouse tent to look at the sea. Several large pieces of ice sat squarely on the eastern side of the search area. "Damn ice,"

57

growled Phil, "it's everywhere, cutting off the search path. It's no wonder the ship was crushed by the stuff."

That day Phil and his team steered the Zodiac toward the mouth of the bay and headed southeast towards Cape Riley. We would wait a day before returning to the site where they had made the underwater contact. "Today we should try a long sweep toward the east," said Phil. "If the *Breadalbane* broke up as she sank, some of her timbers might be scattered in that direction."

"In any case," said Doug zipping up his parka, "it will be a relief to run this search ship of ours across open water. Without the ice in our way we should be able to cover a lot of sea floor."

We watched them pull away from the shore and head out to sea. All of us hoped that by noon the ice might drift away from the area south of the island, the area we really wanted to search.

But the hours of sweeping the sea were unproductive. Returning to shore, Phil's crew had nothing to show for their voyage except five meters of beautifully printed, empty recording paper.

"A good try," he said, warming his hands over the cookstove. "The side-scan is working well. We also know one thing for sure. The *Breadalbane* does *not* lie in the area we searched today."

* * * * *

Nightfall comes slowly to a late summer camp in the high Arctic. The confining cliffs around the bay turn black, the sea is cold and bleak, and the only thing familiar to southern eyes are the filmy clouds moving through the sky.

We gathered in the warmth of the longhouse tent to prepare dinner and discuss the day. Two Coleman lanterns burned brightly at either end of the tent. A round of drinks was poured, the occasion enlivened by the surprise arrival of two old friends who had flown in by helicopter from Resolute Bay.

George Hobson, white-haired, his face always crinkled with a smile, is the genial director of the Polar Continental Shelf Project, the Canadian government's scientific support arm in the high Arctic. For years, George and his staff have provided logistic support for hundreds of scientists working in the far north. He was one of our major supporters.

Standing beside George, his face warm in the glow from the lantern, was Maurice Haycock. "Can't tell you how pleased I am to be with you boys," he grinned. "You've finally done it. Put together a team and started the search. I know you'll find her."

Earlier in the day, Maurice made an oil sketch of the Franklin cairn atop Beechey Island. This cairn, built in 1846, had given up no secrets

—despite much anxious searching through the rocks, no records of the Franklin expedition had ever been found in or near it.

The evening was festive. Phil and Doug were still thawing out from their hours in the Zodiac. Old hands at hardship, they were their usual selves, wisecracking, filling the tent with easy laughter. "Bloody cold out there," said Doug. "A good day for some anti-freeze in the blood stream. Like a quart of Johnny Walker."

Rick and Bruce were happy with the results of the day's filming. Making use of George Hobson's helicopter, they had obtained some spectacular aerial views of the island and the ice. Like the rest of the men gathered in the tent, they were completely relaxed, just glad to be here, part of a company of men doing something no one else had done before.

CHAPTER SEVEN

M ost of the next morning was spent setting up the underwater television system. The side-scan equipment was taken out of the Zodiac and replaced by a closed circuit television system. It included a small camera inside a pressure-proof housing, a surface television monitor and one hundred meters of cable. The side-scan was powered by a twelve-volt car battery, but the TV system required 110 volts at sixty cycles. Needing more room, we placed the television system in one inflatable boat and a small Honda generator in the other. Everything was wired up and tested.

After lunch we lashed the two Zodiacs together and eased away from the shore. Fortunately, the sea was calm. We set our course due south, steering between the ice pans, the two Mercury outboards purring quietly behind us. Moving through the water slowly, we navigated our ungainly craft by speeding up one motor or slowing down the other. With great caution we wound our way out into the Strait, staying well clear of the jagged floes piled up high beneath Beechey's cliffs.

Suddenly shouts came from both boats. A cluster of hands shot up and pointed in the same direction. Thirty meters away, a massive white head surged forward out of the water.

The bear swung towards us and glared. His eyes were black and depthless. A thin trail of mist flared from both nostrils. He moved smoothly through the water, propelled by huge strokes of his shovel-sized paws. Those paws, with their razor-sharp claws, would take only seconds to shred a Zodiac.

Something inside of me, something that went back to the Pleistocene, began to shudder. It was the raw fear of being vulnerable and open to attack. Here was the king of the Arctic, one of the few creatures on earth that hunt men for a meal.

We slowed both motors, staying well back from the bear. He was headed west, across our track, on a long swim across the bay from Cape Riley to the southern tip of Beechey Island. He must have been in the water for almost an hour, his hot blood protected from freezing by thick layers of fur and fat.

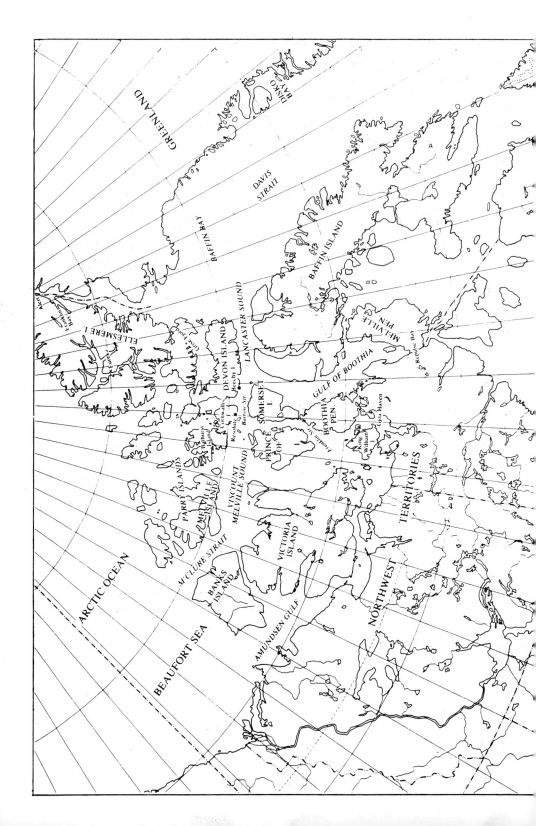

We watched the great bear cruise in towards the shore. As the water shoaled under his big paws, he began to rise out of it, shuffling forward, water streaming down his massive flanks. I pictured the long line of teeth tearing with ease through the flesh and bone of an arm or a thigh. Free of the sea, he turned to face us and shook his great barrel body in the air. For a few seconds he was surrounded by water and splintered prisms of light. He paused and shook again. Then with a sharp sideways glance he turned and padded down the narrow beach.

Each of us made a hard, mental note: a polar bear had landed on our island. Our four square kilometers of treeless terrain had a new land-lord. He could walk to the tents in less than an hour. If he was hungry, he could scoop a razor-sharp claw beneath a tent flap in search of human flesh. A collective sigh was released from the boats. He was headed away from the campsite. But none of us knew for how long.

We continued to motor seaward, circling the smaller ice pans, making a large loop around a flotilla of half-submerged ice. By lining up Beechey's cliffs against landmarks on the inner bay, we manoeuvered into the approximate area where Phil had made his earlier side-scan contact.

We stopped and lowered the television camera and its underwater light, meter by meter, into the water beneath the boats. For the first fifty meters of descent, the screen was grey and lifeless. Then, as the camera neared the sea floor, it flickered and focused on a stunning image.

The sea floor was crowded with life. Between small rocks and pebbles lay clusters of anemones — small flower-like creatures with tentacles waving in the current. There were mussels, clams and star-fish. The camera held its position for a moment and then, as we drifted, it swung away, bringing a new section of sea floor into focus.

Another field of anemones. Brittle stars, feather stars, sea urchins and sponges. Occasionally, there was a growth of soft coral.

Here, hidden under the ice for most of the year, was a high Arctic pasture. For the moment we forgot the ship.

We ranged back and forth, drifting and motoring, moving deeper into the sleep-walking tempo of the watery world. Phil lowered the camera as close to the bottom as he dared, lifting it carefully when he saw an obstacle. Occasionally, it bumped into a boulder, sending up swirls of sediment. Shoulder to shoulder, our eyes glued to the television screen, we peered into the vast chemical bath of the sea, aware that we were the first to see this element-rich, flowering corner of the Arctic continental shelf.

We looked at the sea floor for more than two hours, but saw no trace of the ship. There were no timbers, no planks, no fallen spars. We pressed forward, back and forth against the current, hoping for a sign, a hint of something made of canvas or wood.

As the day faded we continued to motor slowly over the calm sea, searching. The black cable holding the televison camera hummed quietly through the water behind us. Overhead, golden clouds filled the late afternoon sky above Beechey's high stone ramparts. Thirty kilometers away, across the streams of ice drifting south down Wellington Channel, lay the purple cliffs of Cornwallis Island.

We didn't know it then, but our time had run out. The calm seas around us reflected the last of the good weather. There would be a few more hours of searching, but they would yield nothing but frozen fingers and weary bodies. Finally, in Nature's way, we would be driven off the sea. Two days later the wind built up to thirty knots, screamed in from the west, driving the pack ice before it. In twos and threes, and then in gangs of four and five, the floes came in, surrounding the island. Finally, late in the day, a vast white armada, heavy-edged and noisome, drove in hard against the shore, covering the ocean as far as the eye could see.

We were out in the boats when the wind began its relentless drive from the west. Our two Zodiacs made their way slowly back in towards the camp, winding through the narrowing white channels. "We'd better move fast," said Doug, "or we'll have to haul these bloody boats across the ice on our backs." The Zodiacs laboured through the last kilometer. Finally, about a hundred meters from the campsite, we could go no further. Both Zodiacs were emptied of their equipment, hauled in towards the shore and down the beach towards the camp.

That night we finished off the last of the wine. Tomorrow we would be going home. The wine brought us closer, warming us with its expansiveness, easing defeat. In the light of the lanterns, yellow and flickering against the shadowed canvas walls of the tent, we talked quietly of what had happened and what we had learned. "Can't believe how quickly the ice moved in on us," said Rick. "Now I know how they felt at Dunkirk."

It was a good conversation, each man exploring his own thoughts, telling a joke, or describing his impressions of the great vastness that lay just outside. I quietly excused myself and slipped outside the tent.

Hunching down into my parka, I walked along the edge of the shale terrace, alone with the sound of my footsteps on the stones. Hearing a quiet sniffing behind me, I turned to find Moby, his tail wagging.

Together we walked over to the Franklin memorial. Here is where the journey had begun three years ago. Coming back for another search might be impossible. This year's expedition had taken me away from my family and my work. It had required months of effort. Another expedition meant another proposal, more searching for money, further assistance from dozens of individuals and institutions. Another long year of risk and uncertainty.

Somewhere out in the middle of the bay, the ice stirred. A series of reports, like distant gunfire, shot across the stillness. Then, near the shore, there was a hissing, bristling sound as the ice settled into a new position.

I walked over to the white marble tablet at the base of the Franklin Memorial. The tablet lay in shadow, hard and lustreless like the ice.

"Franklin, Crozier, Fitzjames and all their gallant brother officers..."

Distant names with distant memories. In many ways I owed our being here to these men and what they had endured on these shores.

I turned and looked out at the sea. I had to find the ship. It was not just because I loved the spirit of the men now asleep in the tents down the shore from where I stood. I also loved the spirit of the men who had brought us here. Deep inside, down past the fatigue and frustration, in the place where dreams are kept alive, I knew that somehow I would have to come back. I owed it to the memory of those brave men. And I owed it to myself.

I walked back down the shore to my tent. For a few moments I just lay there, listening to the wind. I couldn't help remembering the final minutes of this year's unsuccessful search. The ice had been crowding in, surrounding the Zodiacs. Phil was standing up, surveying the oncoming armada, and then the men crouching below him in the inflatable boat.

"It's time to go my friends," he had said quietly. "If we don't get the hell out of here right now, in a hundred and twenty-five years they'll be coming to look for us."

"I NEED TO BORROW YOUR YOUR ICE-BREAKER."

CHAPTER EIGHT

A pril, 1979. Eight months passed before I returned to Beechey Island. It was a busy year, full of travel, excitement and hard work. Towards the end, there were months of intense planning for a second expedition. However, at the beginning, I was able to give my full attention to my marine consulting business.

One of my contracts was with Casablanca Films in Hollywood. I worked for them as a science adviser on a two-hour television special called *Mysteries of the Sea.* Narrated by William Holden and scheduled for prime time release on the ABC network, the special was a fast-paced documentary film showing some great underwater adventures.

"It's a dynamite project," said the director Al Giddings, as we talked on board his ship moored in San Francisco Bay. "An opportunity of a lifetime. To record, on film, man's technical advances in the deep and remote ocean."

Al paced the room, seething with energy, chopping the air with his fist. Stocky, muscular, dressed in jeans and an open blue shirt, he was the driving force behind the film. For all the years I had known him, he had dreamed of this project.

"Our budget is a million plus," he said. "We're going to get it all — big sharks, sunken Spanish galleons, treasure, deep diving — and make the screen sizzle for two hours."

For months Al and his dedicated team worked furiously, filming from Australia to the Caribbean. The images built up: the deepest breath-hold dive ever made by a human being, close-up views of the slashing teeth of Great White sharks, the discovery of a treasure ship and its hoard of coins and jewels.

I joined him for some of the shooting. Off sea-swept Cape Hatteras we made a dive in a small submarine and peered through the porthole at a famous Civil War ship, the *Monitor.* She lay on her back, her hull twisted and broken, a victim of the fury of the sea. In the warm waters off Hawaii we watched the drama of the deepest dive ever made by a woman. In the eternal blackness, three hundred and sixty-five meters below the surface, a young marine biologist, Dr. Sylvia Earle, moon-walked across the sea floor in an armoured metallic suit.

However, no matter where I was or what I was doing, my thoughts were never far from the *Breadalbane*.

My work on the ABC special and other projects meant I was always travelling. Wherever I went, I was constantly on the lookout for new ideas and people who might help with the search. By a strange coincidence, I met two of them at the North Pole.

For two weeks I was part of a Canadian government scientific station called LOREX. My job was to dive through a small hole in the ice and film cameras and scientific equipment as they were being lowered into the water.

In Trenton, Ontario, I boarded a Canadian Forces C-130 Hercules aircraft and strapped myself into a tight canvas sling seat. For eight hours we droned northward, my knees jammed hard against the cases and crates of cargo that were piled high against the ceiling.

The man sitting beside me had the face and physique of a pirate. Big and thick-jointed, he stood over six feet tall. A magnificent black beard covered his chin. His penetrating dark eyes were framed by a mat of black hair.

I had known Emory Kristof casually for years, but this was the first time we had worked together. A professional photographer for *National Geographic*, he had roamed the world from Moscow to Vietnam making superb pictures. "He's a pretty wild guy," said one of his associates, "but he gets the job done. Above all, Kristof is a superb photographer."

The thing that set Kristof apart was his love of the sea combined with an extraordinary talent for building remote camera systems. Kristof had taken some of the most arresting images ever seen of the deep ocean.

Two years earlier, in 1977, Kristof worked with a team of scientists in the Pacific west of Central America in the Galapagos Rift Valley. For several weeks they used a small submersible to gain access to the abyssal depths where the earth's crustal plates are inching apart. Kristof dropped his cameras into three thousand meters of water, down near cracks and fissures where mineral-rich water was boiling into the frigid sea. He wasn't certain what he would find. He was only sure of one thing — he wanted pictures of the place where the earth's crust was being born.

What Kristof and the scientists saw changed our concepts of the origins of life. They found deep thermal vents around which a dizzying array of life thrived without the aid of sunlight — huge tubeworms, clams, crabs, sea anemones. The basic food source for the life near the vents was the bacteria which lived on hydrogen sulfide coming up from the centre of the earth. It had always been thought that life on earth was inextricably linked to direct light from the sun through chlorophyll and photosynthesis. Now it was found that a large oasis of life, including new and unusual forms, lived separate and apart from this process, on heat and minerals created when the earth was born. Scientists are still analyzing the implications of this discovery.

After flying all day across the wastes of northern Quebec and Baffin Bay, we landed in Thule, Greenland, the big U.S. Air Force base. Built during the Second World War, its large grey hangars and long runways were covered with snow. The next morning we took off again. We headed north across the ice fields of Greenland to the upper end of Ellesmere Island. Approaching its coast, we circled and then landed near a tiny cluster of orange-red huts, the northernmost outpost of civilization in North America. The North Pole was still eight hundred kilometers away.

Alert is a Canadian Forces base that keeps watch on the high Arctic. Within its low buildings is some of the world's most sophisticated communication and direction-finding equipment.

Bouncing along in the small four-wheel truck that took us from the runway to our quarters, Kristof looked at me and smiled. "Great place for a vacation," he said looking out over the terrain. "No women. Nothing but snow and ice and the occasional Arctic fox."

The driver of the truck turned his head and glared. "Better be careful," I whispered, "the guys up here are pretty sensitive. Every one of them is up here for a six-month stretch."

Life at *Alert* was similar to life on board ship. Isolated, boring and repetitious. The men worked around the clock. The only thing that changed was the weather and most of the time it was awesome. Occasionally a man broke down and had to be sent home.

In self-defence the men developed their own brand of humour and lifestyle. They even had their own language. A bed was a "pit." The "Herkie Bird" was the C-130 that flew in each week with mail and movies. Occasionally it flew in with the "short-timers," people like Kristof and myself.

"I'll be glad to get out of here," said Kristof that night at dinner. We were surrounded by sullen, impassive faces.

"Me too," I replied. "Most of these guys have forgotten how to smile."

Next morning we boarded a Twin Otter and flew north again, over a seemingly endless frozen ocean. Everywhere we looked there were long zig-zag lines of piled-up ice, evidence of constant movement. Underneath a cover of snow the ice groaned and shifted, opened and closed, responding to the push and shove of wind and currents.

71

The Arctic Ocean, the smallest of the world's oceans, is almost completely landlocked. It is surrounded by the continents of Europe, Asia and North America. One of its most unique features is its continental shelves, the submerged shoulders of the continent that start at the shore and slope out into the deeps. Off the coast of Russia, these shelves extend out for more than one thousand kilometers, making them the widest in the world.

Recently, off the coast of Alaska and Canada, these submerged shelves have become the subject of intense geological study. The reason: a growing demand for oil and gas.

Further out, in the direction we were heading, was a feature called the Lomonosov Ridge. The ridge, almost three thousand meters high, spanned the ocean floor between Canada and Russia, passing right next to the North Pole.

The ridge was the primary objective of the LOREX scientists. Stationed on the ice, they hoped to drift over it and penetrate its geological secrets with scientific instruments. They were honest scientists doing basic geophysical studies. But somewhere in their findings might be clues to future discoveries of petroleum.

One morning, in a small insulated hut at one end of the LOREX camp, I helped Kristof lower his sophisticated camera through the ice. It was housed inside a long stainless steel tube. Around it was a lattice-work of metal, electronics, timers, and a strobe light. The camera was heavy. Sweating and cursing, we pushed it over the small hole in the floor that led down through the fathom-thick ice.

"Damn," said Kristof, jerking his hand back from the camera. "It bit me." Blood began to ooze from beneath his fingertips where they had been jammed against the edge of the ice hole. Calmly he leaned down and dipped his hand in the freezing water. Then he put his fingers into his mouth.

"Emory," I asked, "have you ever thought of doing something else? Like studio photography, with beautiful women coming to an apartment on Park Avenue."

"I might ask you the same thing," he grinned. "Why aren't you the proprietor of a psychiatric practice for the rich and elderly? Don't answer. We do what we do for honour, fame and the certainty that it will not make us rich."

We watched in silence as the camera slipped through the thin film of ice crystals covering the water. There was a hissing sound as trapped bubbles of air escaped upward. Emory leaned over to watch his camera descend through the brilliantly clear water. "Go baby go," he whispered hoarsely.

It took more than an hour for the camera to descend through the towering column of water that separated us from the sea floor. Outside the building, the temperature was forty below. Inside, it was seventy above. Standing in our shirtsleeves, we sipped coffee and talked.

"I think you've heard that I've got this ship I'd like to find." I said.

"Somewhere in the Northwest Passage isn't it?"

"Yes," I answered, "not far from Resolute Bay. Last summer we had a go at finding her. I think we were getting close. Then the ocean slammed a door of ice in our faces."

Emory sat silently, looking down at the small pool of water rimmed with white crystals.

"You need an ice-breaker," he said, "something to keep the ice open so you can do your work."

"You're right. For the past few months I've been talking to Dome Petroleum who are working in the high Arctic. They're building a new ice-breaker. Sometime in late summer it's going through the Northwest Passage. Right past Beechey Island. How'd you like to join us?"

"Great," boomed Kristof. "You get the ship and I'll get the sidescan. I'd love to join you. And I'll bring along an underwater camera just in case we find it."

From that moment, Kristof's energy and enthusiasm added another dimension to the search. He became devoted to it. He thought about it, worried about it, and drove the project forward.

Far below, Kristof's camera finally reached the sea floor. It was the first of several descents that it would make before the expedition was over. Suspended in the blackness, it began to flash its strobe-light. A piercing yellow beam suddenly illuminated the sediments. One of the pictures Kristof took was of a small pink creature, shrimp-like, walking on wire-thin legs. This tiny blush of colour, strolling across the ocean's basement at the top of the world, confirmed the tenacity of life and its three-billion-year-old wanderings.

In between camera lowerings, Emory and I made a series of dives beneath the ice. On several of these we were joined by Al Giddings who had flown north to the Pole to film a segment for *Mysteries of the Sea*. Once again there was the crystalline clarity and deep purple depths I had seen on my first trip to the Pole in 1974. Once again there were huge tumbled blocks of ice rammed deep into the sea. Returning from my last dive, I noticed a tiny crack leading out from one edge of the ice hole. It nearly spelled disaster for the station.

In mid-April, the ice beneath LOREX split open. There was a muffled thunderclap of sound as the ice shifted and separated. Where there was once a fathom of flint-hard ice, there was now an open lane of motionless black water.

Several hundred meters in length, the crack ran through the centre of the camp. Some of the huts and tents almost toppled into it. For several days it stayed, neither shrinking nor growing, a constant reminder of the temporal existence of those who dwell on the ice.

"Damn thing just missed hitting our science hut," grumbled Steve Blasco, one of LOREX's scientists. "A few more meters and the sea would have swallowed us."

Short, heavy-set, and dark-featured, Blasco was a geophysicist. His passion was the history of rocks: how they bend, fold and fault. His involvement with the Arctic began at Queen's University. Summer studies on the Great Lakes and the Beaufort Sea hooked him forever on the history of sediments lying beneath the Arctic Ocean.

The oil companies were also interested in those same sediments. Long ago, in the croaking gloom of the Carboniferous period, a delerium of trees, vines and organic muck flourished at the mouth of the Mackenzie River. Oil company executives wanted to believe that, as a result, enormous reservoirs of hydrocarbons lay hidden beneath the arctic sediments. Steve Blasco knew a great deal about these sediments and the permafrost, gas hydrates and pingos within them. He began getting phone calls from Calgary and Houston.

"I'm a Quaternary geophysicist," he said proudly as he showed me some of the scientific equipment, including graphs and recorders, that lined his small hut. That meant he studied those misty periods of time that ranged from the present back through almost two million years.

"The clues are in the sediments," said Blasco, pointing at a chart that showed layers of the sea floor's uppermost rocks. Armed with these three-dimensional charts, he was able to make physiographic journeys into the heart of the earth. Like his associates, he spoke with such passion for his subject that it seemed he had been there, somehow projecting himself into the earth.

It was a remarkable achievement, something that comes after years of study and work. It was a particularly impressive feat for Blasco. Some years ago he began having trouble with his eyes. In spite of the best medical help, the retina in both his eyes were disintegrating. Behind the wide smile and warm sense of humour, Blasco was going blind.

One night after dinner, we shrugged into our parkas and went back to Blasco's hut for a drink. A slight wind was blowing across the ice. Even though it was well past nine o'clock, the sun still circled in the sky. At this time of year and at this latitude, the sun was visible twenty-four hours a day. At the entrance to Blasco's hut hung a small, hand-painted sign: POLAR BAR AND GRILL. Once inside, after we had thrown our parkas on a bunk, Blasco offered me a glass of port followed by a small plate of smoked oysters.

"Back home, I tell everybody about the hardships of Arctic science," he laughed. "Up here I try my best to be as comfortable as possible."

After we had talked for a while, I asked Blasco a question that had been haunting me for months. "Last summer, south of Beechey Island, we saw some pretty deep scour marks made by ice in the depths where we hope to find the *Breadalbane*. Some of them were in seventy meters. Any idea how long ago they were made?"

Steve looked at me and smiled.

"You just asked a million dollar question. One that is costing a lot of money to answer. The truth is, no one knows."

"But a lot of people would like to," I said. I knew that oil companies were concerned about big icebergs tearing through the sediments and ripping up buried pipelines.

"In the central Arctic, near Beechey Island, bottom scours could be very recent or very old."

"Can you be more specific?" I persisted.

"Fifteen thousand years old. Or perhaps only a hundred."

"That's a great help," I said, taking a long drink. I was hoping he would say the scours were very old. Old scours would have been made before the ship went down.

"Only one way to find out," said Blasco. "You need a closer look. With side-scan sonars, coring devices, the works."

* * * * *

By June 1979, plans for the second expedition were gaining momentum. Kristof had convinced the National Geographic Society to provide additional support. He also introduced me to Marty Klein, another individual who would make a vital contribution to the *Breadalbane* search.

Klein is a businessman and inventor who has developed the world's most advanced side-scan sonar. Starting as a student at the Massachusetts Institute of Technology, he learned underwater physics and electronics from the legendary Doc Edgerton. By the mid 1960s, Marty was on his own, working in his garage, building an instrument that would give the clearest definition of objects hidden on the sea floor. When I met him, his company, Klein Associates, had a world-wide reputation for superior equipment and skilled people who operated it in the field.

"I know what it's like to struggle against the odds," he said. Pensively he stroked the thick bristles of his black moustache. "You need all the help you can get. We'll give you the equipment and a technician at cost."

"That's really great, Marty," I said. "It's guys like you who make my expeditions work. By the way, who's the technician?"

"Gary Kozak," Marty answered. "He's the best."

75

I had heard of Kozak. He had a reputation as an easy-going, quiet-spoken, hard-drinking individual who could find anything in the sea.

I called Phil Nuytten to tell him how we were approaching this year's search. "Sounds great," he said. "Klein's side-scan is the best. Your new association works out well for us too. Our own equipment is tied up this summer on a long-term contract."

Finally, as the expedition drew near, I went to Calgary to talk to Gordon Harrison, vice-president of Dome Petroleum. Tall, youthful in appearance, Harrison was responsible for the company's two hundred million-dollar off-shore drilling programme. It was Harrison who decided how the company's brand new ice-breaker would be deployed.

One hot summer day, we sat in his corner office that overlooked the building boom in downtown Calgary. "Sure we'd like to help," he said quietly from behind his enormous desk. "We'll arrange to have the ship meet you in Resolute Bay."

Harrison spun his chair around and looked out the window. In the distance were the snow-capped Rockies. "I have to warn you," he said. "The ice-breaker is heavily committed in the Beaufort Sea. We've got to get her there in a hurry."

Harrison turned and looked directly at me. "Can you get your job done in two days?"

Not a chance, I thought to myself, unless we're unbelievably lucky. If it's flat, calm and there's no ice, well maybe. If there's any ice it could take much longer. I decided to gamble.

"I think so," I said, trying to sound optimistic. "It's a short time, but we might be lucky. Let's give it a try."

By the last week in July the expedition was ready to go. Everything was in place except enough money. However, by keeping the search team and its equipment to a minimum, we would make it. Only three of us would go: Kristof, myself and Kozak. We would take only the most essential equipment: the search gear and a few cameras. For the second year in a row there was not enough money to rent a horizontal positioning system. We would have to rely on the ship's officers, working with sextants from the bridge, to fix our position relative to the shore.

The weeks slipped by. The launching of Dome's new ice-breaker was delayed until the middle of September. Word came out of the North that the Arctic summer was short and cold. Winter was coming in early. By the time the ice-breaker started north on its journey through the Passage, the ice had already started to build across Barrow Strait and Lancaster Sound.

On the 19th of September, we boarded a Nordair jet and headed north for a rendezvous in Resolute Bay.

76

CHAPTER NINE

September, 1979. It was the 21st day of September. I was sitting inside a low frame building on the northern outskirts of Resolute Bay. Only one road went beyond this end of town; it led straight to the garbage dump. Grey clouds plodded over the nearby hills and then out to sea. Outside, the temperature was well below freezing. Snow drifts blanketed the ground.

Across the table, staring out the window and then down into the thin wisps of steam curling up from their coffee cups, were Emory Kristof and Gary Kozak. The dankness of ancient sweat hung in the air. From the next room came the murmur of a radio. For the past ten minutes not a word had been spoken.

Somewhere to the east of where we sat, an ice-breaker was beating her way west through the sea-ice of Lancaster Sound. Filled with scientists studying the performance of her maiden voyage, she was racing the end of the season, trying to get through the Northwest Passage before the ice closed it down.

Her name was *Kigoriak*, an Eskimo word for "northern lights." Almost a month behind schedule she was launched in Saint John, New Brunswick, an old maritime port famous for its nineteenth century wooden ships. After a series of short sea trials, her captain, Clive Cunningham, pointed her spoon-shaped bow toward the Arctic. He pushed her hard, driving her nine thousand tonnes up past the tortured coast of Labrador and then, following the old explorers' route, up into Baffin Bay and west into Lancaster Sound. At Pond Inlet he loaded fuel and, with the engines at full power, headed towards Resolute Bay.

The three of us looked up in unison as a gust of wind rattled the window panes. There was the faraway sound of a door slamming shut and boots being stamped clear of snow. "Relax Joe," said Emory, his voice trying to be comforting. "There's nothing we can do except wait. According to the radio, the ship is making good time."

I looked over at the orderly pile of boxes, bags and camera cases next to the door. They were a fraction of the equipment we had hauled to Beechey last year. This time we limited ourselves to an amount that could be ferried out to the ice-breaker in three helicopter loads. Within an hour we could be on the ship and steaming towards the island.

From somewhere came the muffled whap-whap-whap of a helicopter. Kristof's chair fell over backwards as he lunged for the window. A Jet Ranger helicopter, its blades whirling furiously, was hovering over the building. It began to descend. Nearing the ground, it kicked up thin slices of snow and flung them at the window.

A minute later the door to the building swung open and a heavy-set man in a thick orange parka stepped inside. Scowling, he brushed the snow from his arms and stamped his boots. Then he turned to me.

"You MacInnis?" he asked, his voice metallic. "The name's Kennedy. We just had a meeting on the ship to talk about your search project. We won't be able to help you. There's a lot of ice west of here and we've got to keep moving until we get past Viscount Melville Sound."

Kennedy's words hung in the air. I sat down, shaking my head in disbelief. With shaking hands, I reached across the table for my cup of coffee.

"Very well," said Kozak languidly, "we have two alternatives. We can hi-jack the ice-breaker or offer ourselves to the nearest polar bear."

I tried to stir my mind from its numbness. The next scheduled flight back to southern Canada did not leave for two days. We had no ice-breaker. We were trapped in Resolute Bay. Well, I thought, the next few hours are taken care of. We can talk to the men coming off the ice-breaker. And then, when the Arctic Circle Bar opens up, we'll go down there and get roaring drunk.

Twenty minutes later the helicopter came in again. Among the passengers were John and Kathy Lackie, two old friends who were making a documentary film about the ice-breaker's maiden voyage.

"Sorry about the news," sympathized John over a fresh cup of coffee. "Wish there was something we could do to help."

"Awful shame," said Kathy, trying to console us. "You guys have come all this way..."

"The way of the Arctic," I said, trying to sound philosophical. "Part of the agreement."

Blasted ice, I thought, once again it's the blasted ice. If we go back home without putting the search gear in the water, that's it. There won't be another chance.

Kristof stood up, towering over the table. "To hell with it," he said, his voice rising. "Let's have a wake. A bottle of Demerrara, one for each man." He stomped over towards the door and began to pull on his boots.

Kozak eyed me with a malevolent grin. "May as well," he said. "No reason to stay sober."

As I headed for the door, I overheard Kathy talking to John.

"Does Joe know about the other ice-breaker?"

I stopped in my tracks. "What did you say?"

"The other ice-breaker."

"Which one?"

"The big red and white one anchored in the bay."

Sounds like a Canadian Coast Guard ship, I thought. Perhaps it's here for a day or so. If only I could talk to the captain. I turned around. Kennedy was having coffee with three of his men at a small table in the corner.

"Can I use your chopper for a few minutes?" I asked. "I'd like to take a run out to the other ice-breaker."

"No problem," he said. "It'll be free after the next trip. We'll radio the ship and let them know you're coming."

Thirty minutes later we climbed into the helicopter. Kristof and Kozak came with me. They could answer technical questions about the search equipment. "It's a bloody relief to be going somewhere, doing something," growled Kristof from behind his parka hood.

The helicopter lifted off, staggered under a gust of wind, and kicked up snow against the building. Then we turned south and headed out toward the sea.

Scanning the horizon in front of the helicopter, I picked out the ship with its bright red hull and white upperworks. It was a Canadian Coast Guard ship. As we flew in closer, a red maple leaf appeared on her white funnel. Across her bow were bold white letters, *Pierre Radisson*.

As we circled the helicopter pad on the ship's stern, I looked down into the icy black water of the bay and recalled some of the dives we had made beneath its surface. We had made our first dives in 1970 off the northeast shore. Further west we had built Sub-Igloo and dived with Prince Charles.

We landed on the helicopter pad and were greeted by the scent of sea air and diesel exhaust. The big ship rolled slightly in the swells coming in from Barrow Strait.

A few seconds later we were following the navy blue sweater of a junior officer through the ship's polished interior. Just below the bridge we stopped at the entrance to a large room. An imposing sign was fixed over the doorway: Captain Paul Pelland.

We entered to find him standing on the far side of the room. He was short, powerfully built, and wearing a dark blue uniform.

"Gentlemen, please come in. Make yourselves comfortable." The voice had a charming French accent.

"Some coffee?"

We said our thanks and sat down in comfortable leather chairs. I tried to explain our situation. He listened quietly, leaning forward, smoking a long cigarette. "It's a sunken ship," I said. "A ship that sank in 1853 off the coast of Beechey Island." For the next few minutes, I told him about the *Breadalbane*. About last year's search and how this year's plans had gone awry.

"It is an interesting project, my friends. But I am still not certain of one thing. What do you want from me?"

"Your ship, Sir."

Slowly Captain Pelland shifted his big shoulders in his chair. He turned and faced me, inhaling heavily on his cigarette.

"I beg your pardon?"

"Your ship, Sir."

He nodded. "I see." He turned to look at us, one at a time. "I see."

"I admire what you're trying to do," he said, "but unfortunately the decision is not mine. My orders come from Ottawa. I suggest you talk to Fleet Operations."

He leaned forward and stubbed out his cigarette in a glass ashtray. "When you talk to them, describe your situation in detail." He paused. "And tell them one more thing. Tell them I would be willing to support you."

Like all centres of government power, Ottawa is a sprawling, amorphous city where progress is measured in memoranda and meetings. Requests to the bureaucracy can take forever to answer. By the time our problem was received, weighed, and understood, the *Pierre Radisson* would be long gone to another assignment.

As soon as we landed back in Resolute, I placed a long distance call to Dr. Art Collin in Ottawa. Art was a former oceanographer who had worked in the high Arctic. Now an assistant deputy minister with the Department of the Environment, he had never lost his appreciation of the risk well taken.

"Are you serious?" he asked. "Do you really mean you'd like to borrow an ice-breaker for a couple of days?"

"I'm dead serious."

I knew that each summer the Canadian Coast Guard sends a small fleet of ice-breakers into the arctic islands. Their main function is to escort merchant ships, cargo carriers and tankers into and out of the small communities that dot the archipelago. From Grise Fjord to Repulse Bay, from Pond Inlet to Pangnirtung, the arrival of the Coast Guard ice-breaker usually means that cargo and fuel ships are not far behind.

The service is vital to the Arctic communities. Once a year, usually in late July or August, a supply ship brings in most of the food, fuel, clothing and other necessities that keep the community going for the next twelve months. The ice-breaker steams in first, cutting a path through the ice that allows the supply ship, usually close behind, to discharge its cargo on shore.

During the summer, the ice-breakers spend part of their time standing by, waiting for the next assignment. Occasionally, they are called on for an emergency airlift or medical assistance. I hoped that the *Pierre Radisson* might be free of any obligation for the next few days.

Normally, the wheels of bureaucracy grind slowly. Sometimes, when least expected, they move with stunning efficiency. Countless phone calls later I had a tentative agreement. The Coast Guard would try to help us. We were told to wait in Resolute Bay until further notice.

Two days later, the *Pierre Radisson* weighed anchor and steamed out of the bay. She had been assigned to assist a merchant vessel off-loading supplies on Little Cornwallis Island.

Three days later, the phone rang outside my room. I raced down the hallway and picked it up before the third ring. It was a telegram from the Director of Fleet Systems:

> "The Canadian Coast Guard agrees to place the *Labrador* at your disposal for a twenty-four hour survey in the area of Beechey Island on condition that the MacInnis Foundation pay incremental costs for use of the vessel. These costs, which will be mainly for fuel, are expected to be between five and nine thousand dollars per day depending on the amount consumed. The *Labrador* is at Pond Inlet and could arrive Resolute Bay late the twenty-seventh or early the twenty-eighth. Please confirm by telex if you agree to these conditions."

J.Y. Clarke

My heart sank. Where would I get such a large sum of money? I paced up and down the corridor. Then I placed a long distance call to Calgary.

It took me ten minutes to get through. Gordon Harrison was busy at a top level meeting of Dome's executives. As I explained the situation to him, I could hear his quiet breathing at the other end of the phone. Then there was silence.

"Okay," he said, "we'll help." There was a hint of a laugh. "After all, we did leave you stranded."

Four days passed before the *Labrador* reached Resolute Bay. During that time the wind drummed in steadily from the north. Snow continued to pile up against the sides of the building. Out at sea, endless grey waves pressed against lustreless floes of ice.

We had nothing to do. We moved from our bunks to the dining room and back to our bunks. We talked. We read everything in sight. We looked at the colour-splashed pages of erotic magazines until the pictures became meaningless. Day and night, in a nearby room, a lonely television set flickered out commercial messages from the south.

Nothing offered solace. Each night we trudged through the snow drifts and darkness to the Arctic Circle Bar. For a few hours we joined the rest of the community, surrounding ourselves with the illusions of alcohol.

Much of our time was spent talking and trading anecdotes. Kozak emerged from behind his shyness as a skilled ship-searcher, stubborn and passionate about his work. He had been everywhere, from the Pacific to the North Sea, in pursuit of objects lost beneath the sea.

"The floor of the ocean is littered with shipwrecks," he said one night at the bar. Layers of smoke filled the room. "Until recently, we couldn't get at them. But side-scan sonar and magnetometers have changed all that."

The talk turned to the Spanish bullion fleets that had travelled between America and Spain in the sixteenth and seventeenth centuries. "Those old galleons were loaded with gold, silver and pearls," said Gary.

"How come you're not down in the Florida Keys looking for one of those ships?" asked Emory.

"That part of the world has attracted a different breed of searcher," answered Gary. "All of them obsessive. Some of them crazy."

The Florida Keys are a long string of islands and reefs running southwest of Miami. Since World War II they had been a mecca for treasure divers — a strange community of tough, brawling men who thought nothing of selling their homes and leaving their wives. The only thing that mattered was the dream. Of gold and silver, suddenly uncovered in the sand. In a watery world where few laws applied, these outlaws fueded, lied and cheated. Occasionally they tried to kill each other. Once in a while, one of them discovered a sunken ship worth millions.

"I prefer to spend my spare time in Lake Erie," said Gary. "It's got a different kind of treasure."

Lake Erie is the smallest of the Great Lakes, a shallow wave-tossed stretch of water lying between Canada and the United States. It is famous for its sudden storms which have claimed many ships. For the past three summers, Gary had been living in a small town on its southern shore. Each day he started up his small cabin cruiser and headed out into the open, wave-tossed reaches. In bad weather and good he was out on the water, alone, running his side-scan sonar across the bottom.

"Lake Erie is not like Florida," said Gary, draining his glass. "It's cold and unpredictable. But at least there's not a treasure diver hidden behind every coral head."

"You mean you go out each day *alone?*" I asked.

"Yup, the only way," he answered matter-of-factly. "When you're alone there are no arguments."

"What have you found?" asked Kristof, moving in closer.

"About ten wrecks," smiled Gary.

I asked him how he confirmed what showed up on his side-scan sonar.

"I dive down and check it out."

"Alone?"

"Alone."

I pictured him down in the gloom, swimming by himself, gliding across gaping holes and shadowed decks.

"On one dive," he continued, "I saw a two-masted schooner. She went down sometime late in the eighteenth century. But I'm looking for something more valuable. A cargo ship. Loaded with silver and zinc."

Gary got up from the table and went over to a jukebox standing squarely against the wall. He punched in his quarters and waited.

When the music started to blare, Gary came back to the table.

"How about another round?"

"Sure Gary, this one's on the *National Geographic.*"

Late on the 27th of September the Canadian Coast Guard ice-breaker, *Labrador*, turned into Resolute Bay and dropped its anchor. A small red and white helicopter lifted off its deck and headed across the water towards Resolute. Less than an hour later, we were on board with our equipment. Doffing our parkas, we went below to meet the captain.

The *Labrador* was the oldest ice-breaker in the Coast Guard's fleet. Built in 1953 she had a long history of service, first with the Royal Canadian Navy and, since 1958, with the Coast Guard. For over twenty years she had spent each summer in the Arctic, escorting ships, maintaining aids to navigation, assisting in the making of hydrographic charts and participating in search and rescue missions. One summer she rammed through the Arctic ice until she was only one hundred kilometers from *Alert*, the Canadian Forces base on the northern tip of Ellesmere Island.

The *Labrador* was seventy meters long and displaced over seven thousand tonnes. She was crewed by fifty-five men. Walking through her shining interior towards the captain's cabin, I felt the hum of her six main engines. At full speed, they drove her through the water at sixteen knots.

Captain Claude Green welcomed us into his stateroom. The room smelled of comfortable old leather.

"We're happy to be able to help you out," Green said with a smile. "I'd suggest you use the sick bay to set up your search equipment. It's near the stern of the ship. Our people will give you a hand. As soon as we get to Beechey Island, we'll be ready to start towing."

Soon after, the *Labrador* was steaming out of the bay. A line of broken ice rimmed the southern horizon. Making our way east along the limestone headlands of Cornwallis Island, we passed an embayment in the coast. A series of white-topped waves broke on the stark foreshore. It was Assistance Bay where, in 1850, three ships had wintered over during the search for Sir John Franklin.

Franklin's 1845 expedition was so well supplied with food and other provisions that the British Admiralty waited three years before sending out the first relief expeditions. The plan was to conduct a three-way search. Ships would be sent to the eastern and western Arctic approaches and an overland expedition would come in from the south.

Two ships, commanded by James Clark Ross, headed for Lancaster Sound. Two more, commanded by Kellett and Moore, sailed around South America and then up towards Bering Strait. The overland expedition which went down the Mackenzie River, was commanded by Sir John Richardson. One year later, all three expeditions returned to England. Not a trace had been found of Franklin or his men.

Concern turned to alarm. In 1850 six search parties were sent out, three of them privately financed. Two Royal Navy ships under M'Clure and Collinson, headed for Bering Strait. Six other Royal Navy ships under Austin sailed into Lancaster Sound. That summer, fourteen vessels were probing the Arctic waters.

The first clues to Franklin's fate were discovered near Beechey Island. Captain Ommanney of HMS *Assistance*, searching the foreshore of Devon Island, found evidence of human habitation. Soon after, the remains of Franklin's first winter quarters were found on Beechey Island. The news spread and within weeks ten ships, sails furled, were anchored in Erebus and Terror Bay.

As night fell, the *Labrador* pushed eastward through the darkness. Sometime around midnight the ship drove hard into a huge river of pack ice that had come down from Wellington Channel. The engines slowed. A series of line squalls slammed in from the north, bringing snow. In the driving blizzard, the visibility in front of the ship's bridge fell to less than fifty meters.

For the rest of the night the *Labrador's* steel hull hammered and pounded against the growing weight of the ice. When the ship broke into a small area of open water, the sounds grew distant and almost disappeared. Then there was a loud crash and the scream of ice against metal as a huge block scraped down the length of the hull. Just before dawn, the *Labrador* came to a complete stop.

Conscious of the sudden silence, I dressed and made my way up to the bridge. Except for one man standing in the shadows, the large room with its wide sweep of windows was empty. In the centre of the bridge a line of dials and gauges glowed red. Slowly the officer on watch lifted his binoculars and scanned the horizon.

As I walked quietly across the floor, he spoke without lowering the binoculars.

"We shut her down last night because of the snow squalls." The voice was flat, empty of emotion. "No sense trying to bang through this stuff unless you can see. We'll wait until the sun comes up."

Just before five o'clock, there were footsteps at the door of the bridge and Captain Green walked in. For a few minutes he stood at the window, unsmiling. Precisely at five o'clock he barked an order. "Six main engines on bridge control."

A few minutes later we were steaming slowly through the broken pack. I walked over to the port side of the ship and pressed open a window. The din was frightening. As the *Labrador* drove through the ice, great slabs and blocks snapped away and were driven deep into the sea. Seconds later they emerged with a hiss and fell tumbling along the side of the ship. The air was filled with thunder.

Later that morning we found ourselves deep inside a field of multi-year ice. Beechey Island was a low smudge on the horizon. In front of the ship was a network of pressure ridges, old ice, jammed together into low hummocks, fused and weathered into submerged white walls.

The ship came to a stop. Captain Green stood at the window, his shoulders squared. An hour ago he had ordered that the ship's heeling system be turned on. Tonnes of water were pumped from one side of the ship to the other, rocking it, loosening the ice pressing against the hull.

This time the heeling system was not having any effect. The *Labrador* had smashed hard into a thick old ridge that had stopped the ship cold. It held us securely.

"Full astern and try again."

With an effort the ship backed down, opening a lane of black water between the bow and the ice. Pieces of broken ice boiled to the surface.

"Full ahead."

The *Labrador* picked up speed, charging back up the lane of open water. Suddenly there was a wall of whiteness under the bow. Then a tremendous crash. The bow tilted skyward and Captain Green fell forward and struck his forehead against the glass. He stepped back, unsmiling, dusting a nonexistent speck off his sleeve.

"Full astern and try again."

The old ship backed down off the crown of the ice. Metal and ice shrieked at each other. Its propellers churning, the *Labrador* staggered back down the lane of broken water.

The bridge was hushed. In the distance, Beechey Island's thin grey cliffs had disappeared behind a low cloud. The ship slowed its retreat and paused. Then the engines were pushed full ahead.

The *Labrador* laboured forward, gathering speed. Its two big propellers clawed through the water. When the bow hit the ridge, the ship was doing almost six knots.

A great groan came up from the metal in front of us. The bow tilted upward and then over at an angle. Without warning there was the sound of cannon-shot. A series of thin cracks appeared in the old ice. The back of the ridge had broken. A few more passes and we would be free.

Once again the ship went into reverse and backed away from the ridge. Just before the engines were put into forward, a voice broke in over the bridge intercom. It was the officer on the flight deck. "Captain, helicopter CG-78 has just taken off and is reporting small patches of open water south of Beechey Island."

CHAPTER TEN

L ate that morning we reached the open water south of Beechey Island. The sky over the cliffs was overcast and grey. Near the stern of the ship, in the windswept shadows under the helicopter deck, half a dozen seamen in rumpled overalls and seacoats gathered to help us launch the tow-fish. They shuffled around on the freezing deck, stamping their feet and thrashing their arms in a futile attempt to keep warm.

Most of them were from the Maritimes, on the east coast of Canada. Some were boys, young and fresh-cheeked, others were older with sea-weathered faces.

These were men finishing a three-month tour of the high Arctic. For ninety days they had been away from their wives and girl friends. They were aching to be home. As we approached them, carrying the sleek and sophisticated tow-fish, they eyed us warily.

Earlier that morning I had gone down to the lower deck to speak to the crew. The air of their small, cramped mess-hall was dank and filled with smoke. The men, sitting and standing several rows deep, looked at me impassively.

There was a quiet murmur of approval as I showed them old sketches of the *Breadalbane* and told them that when the ship sank, the crew scrambled over the side and across the bay to safety. "That's not far from where we is right now," said a voice somewhere in the crowd.

For the next few moments I described the side-scan sonar and the technique of towing it. I emphasized how much we needed their help. When I had finished and was turning to leave, a thick voice rolled up from somewhere behind the screen of tobacco smoke. "Let's find the goddamn thing soon. So we can get the hell out of here."

Just before noon the tow-fish, all polished and freshly painted, was lifted from the deck. The men handled it carefully, lifting it over the railing and watching it glide on its water-dynamic wings. It disappeared within seconds. There was a babble of excitement and a low whistle. "Bloody strange way to go lookin' for a ship."

Some fifty meters of black tow-cable were uncoiled and fed over the side. Then the cable was stopped off and tied to a large metal cleat. The men continued to glance over the railing at the sleek object which was following us obediently.

The first line of search ran parallel to the south coast of the island. We were close to the shore, almost in the lee of the cliffs. Steaming forward at two knots the *Labrador* pulled the tow-fish across the sea floor, letting it search ahead with its pulsing electronic eyes. Ten minutes later, we came to a stop. We had run up against the first of the ice.

The ship began to turn. Another search track was run, back through the open water where we had come.

Down in the sick bay, Emory and Gary hovered expectantly over the side-scan recorder. Its quivering pen traced out a flat, featureless sea floor.

"Bloody ice has us boxed in," I mumbled angrily.

"What do you mean?" asked Gary, looking up from the recorder.

"Most of the prime search area is covered. With thick old ice. One end of it seems to be grounded near the shore."

"What kind of ice did you say?" asked Emory.

"Some old multi-year stuff. With new ice forming in between."

"That's great. Just great," muttered Emory.

Earlier that morning I had talked to the *Labrador's* ice observer, Jerry Franco. A short, pleasant man whose function was to analyse the ice surrounding the *Labrador*, Franco sent his reports back to Ottawa. "Tell me straight Jerry," I said, "what are our chances?"

"Not too good," he said grimly. "We've had one of the coldest summers in memory. There are lots of places where last year's ice hasn't melted."

I kept this information from Gary and Emory. As their heads bent towards the paper rolling out of the recorder, I looked around the small room. The sick bay was a haven from the cold and noise of the ship. Table tops and shelves, once the resting place of bandages and iodine, now held Nikons and high speed Ektachrome. The stainless steel operating table, complete with a bank of overhead lights, had been draped with towels and turned into a workbench.

The recorder pen quivered and paused. Gary stroked his chin and ran his fingers over the calibration knobs. He turned one and then another.

"Damn it, something's wrong."

The pen started to run and then fluttered to a stop.

"The recorder's going crazy." Gary's voice was hoarse. "Something's happening to the tow-fish."

I ran out of the room and sprinted towards the stern. The men were clustered at the railing looking down at the boil of the wake. Pans of ice banged into each other and spun in behind the ship as it moved through the water.

"Here she comes again." The Newfoundlander squinted down at the water.

The tow-cable went taut. It was caught on a pan of ice. Somewhere in the darkness below the ship, the tow-fish was rising, pointing its nose towards the surface.

Slowly, under the increasing weight of the line, the piece of ice turned on itself. Suddenly released, the tow-fish plunged back toward the bottom.

Gary appeared at the stern coatless, breathing heavily. For a moment he stood there shivering, disbelief in his eyes.

The *Labrador* came to a stop and we retrieved the tow-fish. Still dripping, it was carried up across the deck and into the sick bay. "It's no bloody wonder our records are so screwed up," said Gary. "The tow-fish has to maintain a constant height over the sea floor. If it rises and falls like that, the image goes to pieces."

Gary did a quick check of the side-scan.

"Is it okay?" I asked.

"So far." The small room was overheated. Gary nervously wiped a small drop of sweat from the end of his nose. "One thing for sure. If the ice chews through the cable, there'll be two sunken objects off Beechey Island."

Our problems grew worse. The wind increased from the east, driving more ice in from Barrow Strait. The small patch of open water almost disappeared. The *Labrador* could break the ice easily, but the pressure of wind and currents kept pushing it in behind the stern. Gary's recordings alternated between stunningly clear images of the sea floor and unreadable patterns. At times, the chunks and pieces of ice behind the ship were so thick that they were edge to edge. The tow-fish cable fought its way through them. Thirty fathoms below, the tow-fish swerved up and down.

"Jeez, look at that."

Emory's voice boomed across the room. The ship trembled faintly as it struck a large pan of ice. Three heads leaned in toward the recorder.

A long line deeply etched in the sea floor, appeared on the paper. A few meters away was another, running parallel. Between them lay a deeply shadowed trough.

"What's our depth?" asked Emory.

"One hundred meters."

"That's a hell of a deep scour."

"Look, there's another one!"

"Imagine what one of those would do to the *Breadalbane!*"

As the day drew to a close, the pans of ice behind the ship were almost edge to edge. At times the cable sang like a guitar string. Repeatedly, as the cable caught on the ice, the tow-fish was driven into sudden upward flight. Gary was shaken. He sat in the sick bay huddled over his recorder, shivering slightly from his repeated forays out on the deck.

He looked up at me with a faint smile. "Don't ever, even in a besotted moment, tell Marty Klein what we are doing to his twenty-thousand dollar piece of equipment."

At ten o'clock, in the last light of a cold arctic sun, we decided to stop. The fish and its electronics were being battered too severely. The deck crew was worn out. The men from the Maritimes, their faces red and raw from the wind, lifted the tow-fish tenderly back on board. One of them ran his big knuckled hand over the areas where flecks of paint had disappeared. "Too bad," he muttered, "let's give her another try tomorrow."

That night, under the colossal arch of the sky, the ship lay becalmed in a narrow laneway between two pale white floes. It was a perfect fit of steel and ice, a natural dock conforming to the ship's length and width.

Ice is not always the enemy. Centuries ago, the first Arctic sailors knew that the same forces which crushed a ship could protect it. Early explorers and whalers, caught in storms off Greenland, sometimes ran their vessels into the lee of an iceberg. Mooring lines were attached as the wind howled overhead. As long as the iceberg did not roll over, the ship was safe. If driven towards shore, the keel of the iceberg would touch bottom long before the keel of the ship.

Later it became common practice to "dock" in the ice. If no natural openings were available, large ice saws and, later on, explosives, were used to blast out an opening in the polar pack. Once the ship was nestled inside, the severity of wind mattered little.

In 1632, Captain Thomas James took an even bolder step to save his ship. The onset of winter found him anchored off a small island in the southern corner of Hudson Bay. Waves were battering his vessel, smashing it against shallow rocks. He unloaded as much of the cargo as he could and hauled it ashore. Then, with fervent prayers to the Almighty, he ordered a series of holes to be cut in the hull down near the keel. His ship quickly sank.

Wedged firmly against the sea floor, with her bilges and lower decks below water, she survived the winter. She was no longer moving and the ice could not crush the lower part of her hull. Late the next spring at low tide, when most of the ice had gone, James and his men repaired the holes, pumped her dry and sailed back to England.

The next morning, right after breakfast, we put the tow-fish back in the water. The *Labrador* had steamed less than a kilometer when a big piece of ice moved into our wake and broke in two. The tow-cable cut deeply into the flank of the larger piece. The water boiled, the cable went taut, and the tow-fish shot towards the surface. Just as suddenly, the cable slipped down the flank of the ice and went slack.

Gary appeared at the stern, chewing on an ink-stained thumbnail. "We need some kind of bridle," he said. "Something to hold the cable closer to the ship. Something to keep it away from the ice."

"Won't it be too close to the props?" asked Emory.

"We have to risk it."

A third voice entered the conversation. "Perhaps we could protect the cable," said the first mate, "by running it down through a small pipe. Let's see if we have a thick-walled pipe somewhere on board."

We pulled the tow-fish out of the ocean and spent the next few hours attempting to rig up a bridle. The ship was searched from stem to stern, but there was no pipe of the right length or diameter on board. Even if we found one, there was no way to attach it securely to the curve of the stern.

We stood on the stern, cursing the ocean and the ice.

"Damn," muttered Emory. "This white stuff is only useful when its mixed in a daquiri."

"I've got an idea," said Bill McQuarrie. McQuarrie, the first mate, was a young man with a neatly trimmed beard. Full of enthusiasm for our project, he was our main link between the captain and the crew. "Let's sling a pair of wires under the stern and run it through."

The wires were found, cut, shackled and hoisted over the side. Then they were drawn tight. The plan was to force the cable into the water just aft of the propellers. The wash from the propellers would keep the ice away and the cable running free.

Gary took off his glasses and began to rub them vigorously. "If the ship stops suddenly," he said, "we'll sever the cable."

Positioning the bridle near the midline of the ship was a delicate operation. Someone had to go over the side and down the sheer of the hull. Two men volunteered. Shrugging into safety harnesses they stepped up to the railing and glanced down at the small patch of water three body lengths below them. Both of them knew what it meant to fall into the sea near the propellers.

One of the men stood up on the railing. The second man followed. Grimacing with effort, they wrapped their gloved hands tightly around the safety line. Slowly they began to descend. A voice came out on the wind from the starboard side. "By all that's holy lads, don'ya slip."

The men worked their way downward, stopping two fathoms above the slow churn of the propellers. For twenty minutes they hung there, safety lines taut, voices warming the air with cursing and laughter.

91

Occasionally the metal wire shrieked as it was cinched against the hull. When the men had finished, they were hauled back upwards. Their faces were crimson.

"That ought to bloody well do 'er, she's tight as a banker's fist."

As the last man climbed over the railing he turned around and spat something white down at the sea. Someone handed him a burning cigarette. He inhaled deeply.

The makeshift bridle did not work. Under increasing pressure from the wind, the ice jammed in closer towards the hull. It hissed and crackled. When the ship moved forward, the tow-cable continued to snag.

Most of the afternoon was spent ramming through the ice at high speed near the mouth of the bay. After several passes, the ice became loose enough to launch the fish. But only for a few moments. Then the ice closed in again.

We continued to go through the motions of a search. The ship moved back and forth in the broken channels; positions were taken from prominent landmarks; the side-scan was raised and lowered; and scattered tracings were recorded and interpreted. We went through the motions, not because we held out much hope, but because we were a group of stubborn human beings caught up in the momentum of trying.

There was another essential thread in the psychological bond that held us all together. No one wanted to voice the words of defeat. None of us, either in the ship's crew or search team wanted to hear the wooden finality of "Let's quit."

The day ended with increasing wind, long lines of snow flurries and a falling barometer.

We ate dinner in the officers' dining room. A wan light edged through the portholes. The room had green carpets, white scrubbed walls and comfortable low-backed chairs. The table was set with linen and sparkling silver. A fragrance of roast chicken came from the nearby galley. "You're certainly looking after us in splendid fashion," said Emory, biting into a freshly buttered roll. Emory, who during a photo assignment in Vietnam had been hit in the eye by shrapnel, was familiar with hardship.

"Sure beats last year," I said. "This time of night we would be cooking freeze-dried food on the beach." Over Emory's shoulder, the porthole grew dark. Snow flurries raced through the air. The steward, dressed in a clean white jacket, entered the room with a steaming plate of potatoes.

"I wish we could find it for you," said Captain Green. He pushed his wire-rimmed glasses snugly against the bridge of his nose.

"If only you'd been with us last month," said the Chief Engineer.

"Most of Barrow Strait was open and clear." I turned my water glass slowly on the white linen tablecloth, watching the lights flicker from its bevelled edges. Inside the glass, two pieces of ice were slowly melting.

"Next year let's arrange something in advance," said Captain Green. He smiled. "Your underwater search is the kind of thing we ought to support. You guys are working with equipment we should know more about."

"I think you're right," I said. "You're one of the few people who recognize that what we are doing goes far beyond the search for a sunken ship. We are really trying to expand the nation's capacity to work under the ice. Even a setback means we've learned something."

The voices of the men rose and fell with the rhythm of individual conversations. Across the table, Emory and Gary talked about the *Breadalbane*. They were continually optimistic. Both of them were ocean-going nomads, their lives having a dynamic all its own. Failure was a part of it, but only temporarily. Wherever they worked, in Lake Erie or the Caribbean, they tried to be as precise as possible in an imprecise world. When physical and chemical laws conspired against them, they resorted to risk. No matter what happened, they would keep trying.

The next morning, our last, we tried to survey the ice-covered waters south and west of the island. "It's the only place where the polar pack can be broken easily," said Captain Green. He surveyed the white rubble field in front of the *Labrador*. "We'll make a few runs to clear a channel and then drop the side-scan."

For several hours the *Labrador* worked back and forth, smashing the new ice and scattering it to either side of the ship. But almost as soon as we passed, the ice moved in to fill the water behind us.

The tow-fish was repeatedly launched and recovered. For a few hundred meters there would be a clean, uninterrupted track. Then, as the pressure built up in the ice around the slow-moving ship, the cable would snag on one of the broken pans. Down in the sick bay, the images coming out of the recorder would disintegrate.

As the morning wore on, the wind increased and the temperature fell. The wind, biting like winter, gusted across the deck, working into the up-turned collars of the seamen on the stern. Their faces were crimson. They cursed and stamped their feet, leaning out over the railing to pull the tow-cable across another large cake of ice.

"Lard Jasus," one of them yelled, "take a look at that, byes."

The tow-fish shot clear of the water. It skidded up the smooth slope of an ice pan and skated across the surface. Wobbling on its wings, it battered itself on the ice and plunged back into the water.

Emory ran out from the sick bay, leaned over the railing and looked down. He closed his eyes.

"Better slow the ship lads or we'll lose 'er."

Three pairs of hands worked furiously to steer the cable around the huge cakes of ice that completely surrounded us.

The tow-fish surfaced and shot sideways. It flipped on its yellow wings, climbed another piece of ice and jammed itself into a crevice. The whole piece of ice began to move.

Seconds later the *Labrador* began to slow as if stopped by an invisible hand. The tow-cable went slack. Leaning forward, Emory opened his eyes. The veins in his temples were coiled like knots.

Two burly seamen reached over the stern and grabbed the slack cable. As they leaned over, a huge block of ice, pearly white and jagged, turned on its side and rose out of the sea. Pushed up by the propellers, it teetered for a moment on its edge. Then it crashed downwards, just missing the men.

Gary appeared at the railing, his arms bare, his face ashen.

"Joe," he said, "there's no signal on the recorder. The fish has gone dead."

* * * * *

As it turned out, the fish had not really died. It was suffering from a temporary concussion. Battered by the ice, its complicated electronics had stopped working.

A few hours later, after crouching over his patient in the sick bay, Gary had things back to normal. But it was too late — the ice had closed in. We would have to wait another year.

CHAPTER ELEVEN

E xactly what happened during the final voyage of the *Breadalbane* will never be fully known. Her logbook, cargo manifest and hull plans have all disappeared. However, with the help of historians at the National Maritime Museum in Greenwich, some old photographs and manuscripts from that period, and the insight of sailor-historian Samuel Eliot Morison, it is possible to imagine life on board a three-masted barque leaving London and crossing the North Atlantic in the spring of 1853.

The *Breadalbane* was a true working wind-ship. She was approximately thirty-eight meters long, had three masts, and displaced four hundred and twenty-eight tons. A single deck ran from bow to stern. On this deck, just forward of her steering wheel, was a flat-roofed deck-house containing a small stove and accommodations for the crew. Below her deck near the stern, were small cabins for the master and the officers. Her hold was filled with stores and provisions: food, clothing, timber, spirits, canvas, line and spare parts.

On May 19, the *Breadalbane* and her consort, HMS *Phoenix*, sailed out from Sheerness at the mouth of the Thames. Deep in the iron belly of the *Phoenix* was a load of coal and a coal-fired steam engine. Buried under her stern was a screw propeller. The *Phoenix* was the first such ship to enter the high Arctic. The Royal Navy believed that she heralded a new era — the age of steam — and that she would be much safer and more efficient in the ice than a wind-ship. She was one of the first real "ice-breakers."

We know from the journal of William Fawckner, the government agent on board, some of the landmarks of the *Breadalbane's* journey. On May 26, after taking on additional supplies and six sheep, the *Breadalbane* slipped out of the harbour at Cork, Ireland, and headed north into the Atlantic. The *Phoenix* had left a few days earlier. Their planned rendezvous was Disko Island, halfway up the west coast of Greenland.

Since the time of the Vikings, sailing ships have followed more or less the same route across the North Atlantic and into the Canadian

Arctic. The first leg of the journey took advantage of the prevailing westerly winds. The ships sailed a long arc north from Ireland to the Hebrides and Faroe Islands and then slanted west towards Iceland. Here, they picked up favourable currents for the westerly passage to the southern tip of Greenland. The "stepping stone" route not only made the most of the currents and winds, but it allowed the ships to make sightings of known island landmarks. It was a hazardous route that offered the security of safe harbours along the way.

The North Atlantic is renowned for its variable weather. There are prolonged periods of overcast skies, rain, high winds and snow. Fine weather is rarely encountered; cloudy skies are the rule. Even in summer the North Atlantic is a sea of storms. Easterly gales bring drenching rains; westerly gales give birth to huge waves. When a northerly blasts in, it hurls a ship southward, claws at her sails, and tries to drive her over on her beam ends.

As the *Breadalbane* worked its way north into higher latitudes, the days grew longer. The ship sailed into the polar world where the summer sun maintains a constant twilight. Looking up at the sky, it was impossible for the crew to tell if it was day or night. The ship sailed on, the weather became increasingly cold; the winds blowing into the sails had the touch of the northern ice.

Even in the middle of the last century, a voyage across the North Atlantic was a risky affair. If a wind-ship was blown off course and set against an unknown shore, its square-rigged sails would not allow it to manoeuvre easily. It could not point up into the wind. In summer, northern coasts were often cloaked with fog. Off every shore were submerged rocks waiting to tear the heart out of a wooden ship. Even from high in the crow's nest, it was impossible to see down through the dark green waters of the North Atlantic.

If a man working near the rail of the *Breadalbane* fell overboard, he had to be rescued within minutes. Otherwise he would perish from the cold. Most of the men could not swim. If someone chanced to fall overboard in a fog, they were lost. The last thing they heard were their own shouts swallowed by the mist.

In Victorian times, most of the seamen in the Merchant Navy were poor and uneducated. Every one of them, especially the captain, needed superhuman will. Daily, they faced the unknown terror of the northern ocean. In those days, in the minds of the men, the ocean deeps were filled with immense creatures and obscure powers.

Days at sea were stitched together by formal routines. The watches were changed, the ship was pumped dry, the wheel was relieved, according to a strict schedule developed over centuries of seafaring. At fixed hours stellar and solar sights were made, the wind and weather noted, dead-reckoning estimated and entry made into the ship's log.

Any departure from an established custom was resented by both officers and crew.

The men of the *Breadalbane* were divided into two watches of four hours each, each watch commanded by an officer. At four, eight, and twelve o'clock, the watches were changed. In the afternoon, the watch was "dogged," (that is, split into two-hour watches), so that the men might change their hours every night. This procedure gave each man the unpopular "graveyard" watch, from midnight to four, on alternate nights.

Time on board the *Breadalbane* was reckoned in terms of watches and bells. Each half hour of the day and night, a series of musical notes rang out across the deck marking the passage of time. They also served to remind the men that safe passage depended on their vigilance and the staunchness of the vessel.

Merchant seamen were pious and devout. Each day they gazed skyward seeking divine protection. Prayers were a part of their daily ritual. Somewhere on board the *Breadalbane*, perhaps in the deck-house so that all could see it, hung a framed copy of the 107th Psalm: "They that go down to the sea in ships and occupy their business in great waters; these men see the works of the Lord, and His wonders in the deep."

Every morning and evening prayers were held, led by the captain or the master. Throughout the day, especially when the ship was threatened, there were semi-religious observances. Holy sayings were often spoken by the youngest lad on board; it was believed that a voice of innocence had easier access to God.

Just before their early morning watch, the men rose from their damp bunks. Many were already dressed; they had not bothered to remove their clothes when they had tumbled into bed at the end of the last watch. On the way aft, each grabbed a piece of ship biscuit, cheese and a slice of pork.

At the change of the watch, the helmsman gave the course to the officer commanding his watch who repeated it to the new helmsman who repeated it again. No chances were taken that an order might be misunderstood. Shortly thereafter look-outs were posted, a caution was given about the weather and the watch-officer noted the ship's estimated position in his logbook. The first duty of the men coming up on watch was to pump the ship dry. The off-going watch slipped down below to eat breakfast before curling up to sleep.

During its four hours of duty, each watch was responsible for the running of the ship. Their tasks included keeping the deck clear and clean, checking that the cargo was securely tied down, making and setting sail, trimming the sheets and yards and overhauling the gear. During a storm, everyone was summoned on deck to help.

The master of the ship remained aloof. It was his responsibility to estimate the weather, the sea-ice and the currents. He had to decide which sails to put up or take down, how the food was to be rationed and, most importantly, maintain the morale of his crew. In the mornings, after a wash in a bucket of fresh water and a bit of breakfast in his cabin, he came up on deck, talked with the officer of the watch and cast his eyes around the horizon.

The master's orders were transmitted to the men through the officer or bo's'n. Around his neck, the bo's'n carried a pipe on which he played a series of signals that, even in the shrillest wind, carried right up to the top-most yard.

Because the *Breadalbane's* deck-house was forward of the steering wheel, it was impossible for the helmsman to see directly ahead of the ship. The officer of the watch, stationed where he could see the bowsprit, conned the helmsman, telling him what course to steer by. In front of the helmsman was a second compass on which he followed the ship's heading.

Meals on board Victorian merchant ships were comparatively good with at least one hot meal a day. Staples of the men's diet, as they had been for centuries, were salt meat, codfish and sea biscuits or hardtack. Usually around noon, at the changing of the watch, a hot meal was served. It was cooked on a small stove in the deck-house and served to the men with a steaming mug of tea.

When men venture far from shore for long periods of time, one of the greatest threats to health is scurvy. Untreated, it is always fatal. Brought on by lack of Vitamin C, it results in painful swollen limbs, bleeding gums, loosened teeth, depression and mental aberrations.

Scurvy was very prevalent at sea between the sixteenth and nineteenth centuries owing to the difficulty of preserving fresh food such as fruits and vegetables. It usually became apparent after about six weeks on a diet of salt meat and biscuits. Because it debilitated crews before it killed them, scurvy was responsible for many shipwrecks, particularly on the long voyages of the East Indiamen or sailing from London around Africa and east to the Orient.

In 1753, one hundred years before the *Breadalbane* sank, James Lind, a Scottish Naval surgeon, published his *Treatise of the Scurvy*, proving that it was a deficiency disease. He argued that oranges and lemons were a cure. Captain James Cook provided fresh food to his crews during three long Pacific voyages and, as a result, did not lose a single man to scurvy. It was an unprecedented achievement. In 1795, the drinking of lemon juice was compulsory and scurvy was almost eliminated from the Royal Navy.

However, during polar voyages, even those made in the early years of this century, scurvy plagued the Royal Navy. It broke out during the

1875-76 North Pole expedition. It enfeebled Scott and his men during their tragic journey to the South Pole in 1911-12.

The problem was that the Royal Navy began to use food that had been tinned and preserved. Economical and convenient, it eliminated the daily source of Vitamin C. As well, lemon juice was bottled under conditions which destroyed the vitamin. Later, lime juice, with half the antiscorbutic value, was substituted for lemon juice. (This is the origin of the American word "limey" for a British immigrant.)

Ironically for Scott, who died on his return from the South Pole, the true cause of scurvy was found with the discovery of vitamins in 1912, the same year he died. Even more ironic was that a thousand years before, the Vikings, on their way to Greenland and North America, had avoided scurvy by eating Arctic cloudberry (Rubus Chameomorus L.). Weight for weight, this small berry contains twice as much Vitamin C as oranges and lemons. Intuitively the Vikings had sensed its life-saving effects.

Every day, a substantial serving of alcohol in the form of beer, wine, or rum, was served to each man from a wooden barrel. At the longed-for hour, the cooper went below to remove the wooden bung from the designated cask. During a storm, especially if a northerly was blowing, he might make several trips.

In those days, many of the men who took to sea were criminals, farmers driven off their land, and down-and-outers. Some were drunkards, men for whom drinking was a way of life. On shore they were found in taverns until their money ran out; on board ship they were first in line for the daily rum ration. The officers kept a close watch on these men; in bad weather they were a liability. Frequently, they were kept away from alcohol for the entire voyage in an attempt to dry them out. Too often their sobriety lasted only until the ship arrived at the first harbour with a tavern.

When he felt the urge, a Victorian sailor simply urinated over the side of the ship. As he ambled toward the railing, he would take care to assess the strength and direction of the wind. In good weather, regular evacuations were performed at the "head" of the ship on crude seats hung over the forward rail. As evening fell, it was a splendid place to contemplate the rising moon and stars. In bad weather, many a bare bottom was stung by the cold lash of a wave.

No one on board the *Breadalbane*, not even the master, was immune to seasickness. Rough weather, especially at the beginning of a voyage before the men had their sea-legs, would incapacitate the strongest man. In a storm, it was not unusual to see a man, his face green, unable to move, lying in his own vomit.

Dead-reckoning was the underlying principle of navigating a square-rigged ship across the North Atlantic. Each day, from noon to noon, the master added up the estimated distances of all the watches, considered the effects of currents and wind-drift, and ascertained as near as possible, his position. On longer voyages, a miscalculation of half a point in the ship's course might mean a land-fall error of hundreds of kilometers. At night, in a fog or storm when the look-outs were unable to see, this often meant disaster.

There was little idle time on board a wind-ship. There was always work to be done; making repairs, splicing lines, seizing rope, scrubbing down. But if a fair wind blew over the stern and the sails needed no handling, the men sat and talked, washed their clothes, whittled, spun yarns or perhaps tended a fishhook. The act of washing one's body in a pail of cold North Atlantic water required considerable courage. It happened seldom, sometimes never, during the entire voyage.

As the weeks passed, the *Breadalbane* made its way north under its press of square sails and three raking masts. Finally it sailed into the lee of Cape Farewell at the southern tip of Greenland. From here the route was the "whaler's route" up the west coast of Greenland, taking advantage of open water and the northbound current.

As the *Breadalbane* headed up the eastern side of Davis Strait look-outs were posted, even at night, for ice and icebergs. Every hour the man on the helm and the look-out were relieved. The officer of the watch paced the deck, keeping an eye on things, checking the compass to confirm the helmsman was holding his course.

Gales were common on this leg of the voyage. Storms usually approached the ship early in the morning under a darkening sky. The men would be hauled out of their beds to lash down everything and furl the mainsails. Despite their preparations, if the storm was severe the first blast of wind heeled the ship, driving it over on its side.

After the wind came the rain, smashing at the deck and then changing suddenly to hail. Thousands of white pellets burst over everything, clattering like marbles down the lee rail. Just as suddenly, the downpour might change back to rain.

Dressed in oilskins, the helmsman and the small knot of men around him averted their faces as the rain slanted in across the deck. Under the helmsman's hands, the spokes of the wheel became cold and slippery, forcing the strength from his fingers.

As the winds increased, the ship gathered speed, driving forward into heaving seas. If it turned broad to the wind, a great wave might roll out of nowhere and break over the windward rail, roaring across the deck, submerging the hatches and swirling into the scuppers.

If the storm was extreme, the topmasts bent like whips. Men were sent up ratlines to cut away a blown-out sail. They had to inch upwards, holding on for dear life as the rolling ship tried to fling them clear. High overhead they fought their way out to the end of the yards,

The John A. Macdonald *during the 1980 search.*
Emory Kristof — ©*National Geographic Society*

The RPV being lowered over the side of the Pierre Radisson *into the freezing waters of the Northwest Passage to get the first close-up views of the* Breadalbane.
Emory Kristof — ©National Geographic Society

The author examines the Klein side-scan sonar prior to launch in 1979. He is on the helicopter deck of the Labrador.
Emory Kristof — © National Geographic Society

From left to right, Maurice Haycock, a crew member, Mike Moog, Joe MacInnis and Gary Kozak on the bridge of the John A. Macdonald *just before the discovery of the* Breadalbane *on August 13, 1980. Emory Kristof — ©National Geographic Society*

The author (centre), Gary Kozak (right) and Mike Moog (left) holding up recording paper scan sonar on which was printed the first reflections from the Breadalbane. *Emory Kristof — ©National Geographic Society*

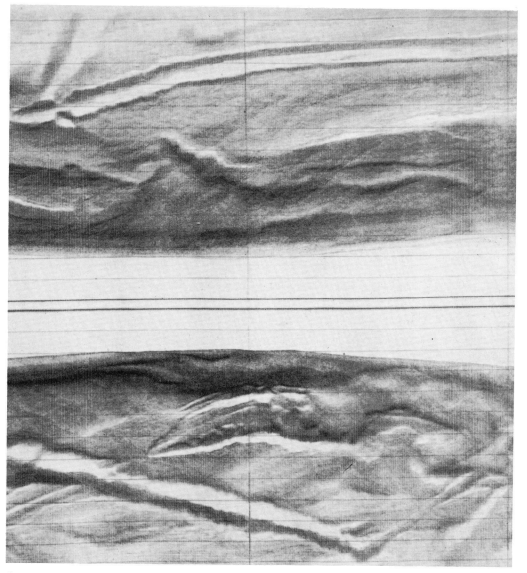

Scours on the sea floor made by down-reaching ice. These scours, and many others not far from the sunken ship, were seen by side-scan sonar.
Gary Kozak, Klein Associates — ©National Geographic Society

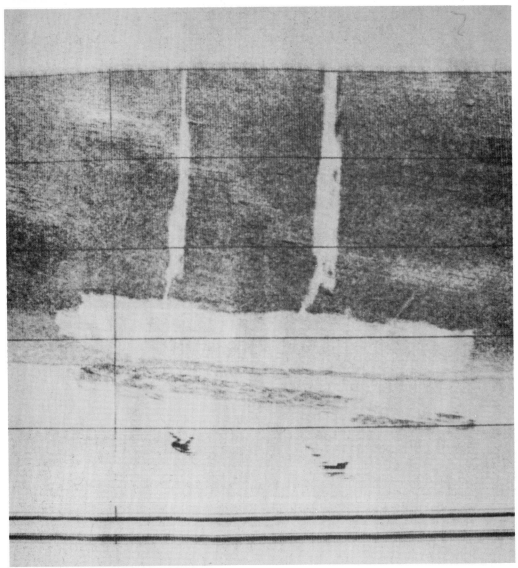

Side-scan sonar image of the Breadalbane *sitting on the sea floor at the moment of discovery in 1980. Two of the masts are still standing and the hull is intact.*
Gary Kozak, Klein Associates — ©National Geographic Society

The spoked wheel of the Breadalbane *is covered by cottony-looking growth after more than a century and a quarter at the bottom of the Northwest Passage.*
Emory Kristof — ©National Geographic Society

The gash in the hull of the Breadalbane *made by the force of the ice in 1853. In the background are fallen timbers covering the cargo.*
Emory Kristof — ©National Geographic Society

Live from the bottom, television cameras reveal the drowned deckhouse of the Breadalbane. *Above the ship's displaced wheel and attached to the deckhouse bulkhead is a storage cabinet containing the ship's compass, a signal lantern, and a navigational instrument.*
Emory Kristof — ©National Geographic Society

Section of one of the Breadalbane's *masts that has fallen clear of the ship.*
Emory Kristof — ©National Geographic Society

slashing away with knives to free the torn strips of canvas.

The men suffered from cold. Fingers became salt-cut and raw, faces crimson. The wind emptied their lungs. The only source of heat was the small coal-stove in the deck-house.

Hours later, the storm would begin to ease. Under torn layers of cloud, the ship would claw its way north through the water. As the light came back into the sky, the look-outs would wipe their eyes and resume the watch for icebergs.

Portions of the personal journal of W.H. Fawckner were reprinted in the *London Illustrated News*, on October 15, 1853. Within them is a telling picture of the last days of the *Breadalbane*.

According to Fawckner, the ship arrived at Disko Island off the west coast of Greenland on Friday, July 8, 1853. At midnight, with the sun still shining, the *Breadalbane* dropped anchor in Lievely, a beautiful little land-locked harbour. The next part of the journey took the *Breadalbane* up the west coast of Greenland to Cape York at the head of Baffin Bay. From there, the plan was to sail west and then south-west, following open water and favourable currents to the entrance of Lancaster Sound.

However, as Fawckner describes it, getting up the west coast of Greenland to Cape York was fraught with difficulties. In spite of this, HMS *Phoenix*, the first screw-propeller ship to voyage into the high Arctic, put on an impressive performance:

"On Saturday, July 9th, the ship was surrounded by ice: The *Phoenix* struck the ice at six p.m., she being then towing the transport. The shock brought both vessels to a stand-still, but, by putting on full power, both vessels managed to get through. The next piece of ice they encountered was fully half-a-mile long and three feet in thickness. The crews of both vessels looked on in astonishment to see the steamer forcing her way through the ice, and crushing it without injuring either ship, although at the time of the concussion they were going at the rate of six miles an hour. Until ten p.m. the vessels were by turns threading and forcing their way through the ice. The sight was both novel and exciting, and officers and men could not forget that had they been without steam, the first ice they took would have been their resting place. At 10:30 p.m., it came on very thick; so Captain Inglefield ran the ships into the ice, and secured them with the ice anchors, where they lay as quiet as if in dock. On the following morning, Sunday, it was discovered that the ice had closed around the vessels during the night. Divine service was performed on board the *Phoenix*, which was attended by the crew and officers of the transport, who walked across the ice. The men from both ships were on the ice in the afternoon. The lowest range of the thermometer was 31 deg. The glare from the ice when the sun shone upon it was so great as to be distressing. Some strange contrasts were observable in the apparel of the voyagers, which would have made a sensation in Pall-Mall; long sea boots, for instance, being worn to keep the feet and legs warm and dry, and upon the heads a straw hat and veil to keep off the sun."

Ice wasn't the only problem. On Monday, July 18, the men of the *Breadalbane* encountered a polar bear:

"The first bear was seen tramping over the ice, and muskets and bullets were immediately got ready to give him a warm reception. Bruin, however, did not come nearer than within a mile. At six p.m., *Phoenix* made another start, with the transport behind; and succeeded, by running full speed at the ice, and by blasting, cutting and clearing it, to get about ten miles by two a.m. (the 19th). Sometimes it would take an hour to clear two ship's lengths; then there would be clear water for a mile or two, when another passage had to be forced, in order to get into clear water again. It was very exciting work. The blasting was found to be of great service; and the spirits of all on board were cheered by the reflection that what they had done in a few hours a sailing vessel would have taken weeks to accomplish. The ice-master, indeed, who had had experience in these waters for twenty years, declared that no sailing vessel could have done it. The way in which the steamer crushed up the ice under her sharp bow — some of it being four feet and upwards in thickness — was wonderful."

Keeping the *Breadalbane* moving through the pack-ice was physically exhausting. In addition to the pulling, lifting and shoving, there was the threat of falling into the water or being crushed. Some men, like Fawckner, were lucky. He fell into the water and, so it seems, hardly got wet. He writes:

"Saturday, July 23. Up to this date we have been daily at work blasting, cutting and clearing a passage for the ship. Sometimes parties have been employed upon the ice tracking the ship (hauling her along by ropes). Since entering the ice this week, the average distance gone each day does not exceed fifteen miles. Today found the ice much thicker, some being from six to seven feet thick. It made the ship tremble in every timber, when running into it. The transport fouled the *Phoenix* once, and did her some damage, knocking her bows about a little. In the afternoon, found the ice too heavy to force a passage, so secured the vessels to it. Three bears were seen about three miles from the ship: a party, armed to the teeth, went after them — of which I numbered one. On approaching them, however, they made off, having thus given us a long tramp for nothing. On returning from the bear-hunt, I was crossing on the ice from one ship to the other, with my gun upon my shoulder, when the ice — being too weak to sustain my weight — gave way, and I was immersed in the water. I easily got out, however, without even the loss of my shooting iron. It was the coldest bath I ever had, and will teach me to be more cautious in future."

For men who were making their first journey into the Arctic, there was much to see and to learn — especially about the ice:

"It is exceedingly heavy and fatiguing work to traverse the ice on foot, or rather the snow, with which the ice is covered. Distance, too, is very deceptive, from the clearness of the atmosphere, every object appearing to be not more than a third of its actual distance. One day during the past week a party started for some small islands which appeared about a mile or a mile and a half distant, but which proved to be quite five. It took them four hours before they returned to the ship, and quite fagged they were when they arrived. They found on the islands a human skull and a bear's head. We have seen and been among a very great number of icebergs, some in very critical positions. When drifting they crush everything before them. Fortunately, it has not blown hard, or we might have had some unpleasant squeezes from the ice. On the 23rd we saw some very large icebergs about a mile in length, and the highest about 400 feet in height. Their depth under water is generally considered to equal to from six to seven times their height."

It took the ships only two days to travel west across Baffin Bay. According to Fawckner, the sea was "smooth as a mill-pond." On July 27, they sighted Cape Liverpool, the southern cape at the entrance to Lancaster Sound. The next day they spotted more polar bears.

"This day commenced with a little sport among the bears. One fellow was making his way towards the ship across the ice; but, on two or three persons landing on the ice from the ship, bruin made off. They cut off his retreat, and the bear then took to the water. The boat chased him, and with one shot he was killed. Two more were shot in the water in the course of two hours. They swim fast, but a good pulling-boat easily overtakes them."

On July 29, with the ice stretching across Lancaster Sound, the *Breadalbane* steered for Dundas Harbour, a small bay in the south shore of Devon Island. Waiting for the winds and current to clear away the polar pack from the Sound, they secured both ships to the ice. They continued hunting, but this time it was for walrus.

"There was a little sport today, in catching, or rather hunting, walruses. They are rather difficult to kill, but a boat from the *Phoenix* succeeded in getting one in an hour. I thought I might as well try my luck, and started in a boat with two fowling-pieces, harpoons, and lances. I succeeded in putting two balls into one big fellow, but that was not nearly sufficient to kill him. We persevered for nearly six hours firing at him, and about twenty shots struck him before we captured him. They often attack a boat, and stick their two fearful looking tusks into her; but the one we caught did not attempt it. It was the hardest work, or sport, I had had for a long time. We were about a mile and a half from the ship, when we captured the walrus, and had to tow him that distance through the water. It required a powerful pulley to hoist it in, as it weighed more than a good-sized bullock. The walrus was no sooner on board, than knives were at work skinning it. The flesh is not unlike that of a bullock; and the flesh of a bear is equally as good as beef."

Slices of bear and walrus meat were cooked and served to the men on the *Breadalbane* and the *Phoenix*. The fare would have been a welcome relief from canned beef or salted codfish. The next day, Saturday, Fawckner walked across the ice to the shore of Devon Island:

"On visiting the shore, found a number of Esquimaux graves, with human bones and skulls in them, which is a proof of natives having visited the place many years since. The graves or stones are built up in the form of a box; within which the body is placed. No hole is dug in the ground, according to the European custom of burial... Walked to the Esquimaux village, a distance of about five miles. Found several preserved meat tins, and various other indications of their having seen Englishmen before, or of the Esquimaux having fallen in with some of the provisions that have been landed in this sound. Their tents present a disgusting sight, from the walrus or seal flesh lying in its blood, and the entrails by its side, close to the beds or skins on which they sleep. The stench of these rude habitations is the most offensive that can be conceived. Their dogs must consume much more than they do themselves, but, when short of food, they often keep these useful animals without anything to eat for a week. Clothing is an object of barter they do not value, always pointing to their own seal-skin dresses, which they think, and perhaps correctly, preferable to ours; but iron-work, particularly knives, is their chief aim. I did not see many spears, but a few rough bows and arrows, so that they must use a great deal of stratagem in hunting and fishing. The smallness of their feet is worthy of notice, the whole of them having much smaller feet than those of any civilised persons I have seen."

On Monday, August 8, three months after leaving England, the men of the *Breadalbane* finally reached their destination. Their arrival at Beechey Island coincided with an important chapter in the discovery of the Northwest Passage. Four years earlier, HMS *Investigator*, under Commander M'Clure, had sailed out from London for the Western Arctic, via Bering Strait. While searching for Sir John Franklin near Banks Island, the ship was beset and eventually abandoned. Some of the men from the *Investigator* made their way east over the ice, to the *North Star*, anchored at Beechey Island. The *North Star* was one of five ships commanded by Captain Edward Belcher. Belcher's squadron was the British Admiralty's last major effort to determine the fate of Franklin:

"At four p.m. passed Cape Riley, and saw the *North Star* beset in the ice, with the whole bay (Erebus and Terror Bay) one mass of ice. Could not get nearer to the *North Star* than one mile and a half. It was gratifying to see the surprise and delight evinced by the officers and crew of the *North Star*. They were at the time employed in sawing a canal whereby the vessel might get out. The saws were immediately dropped, and they ran like madmen to meet us. Much greater delight even was shown by two lieutenants of the *Investigator*, which had discovered the long-sought-for Northwest Passage, and is now 400 miles distant from this. They had travelled the whole of that distance on the ice. They had been absent from England nearly four years; had passed three winters in the ice; and, what was worse, had been for two winters on a reduced allowance of food. Many of her crew have suffered and are still suffering from scurvy. Those in the most delicate state of health were taken to the *Resolute*, which vessel had wintered and was at Melville Island in May last, the Captain (Kellett) of that vessel having communicated with the *Investigator*. The latter is now in Mercy Bay (Baring Island), which formerly bore the name of Banks Land, with very heavy ice surrounding her, and not the slightest chance of her getting out. It is, therefore, supposed she will be abandoned and that the crew will have to travel over the ice to one of the ships in these regions."

The *Breadalbane* was sailing under orders to unload her cargo as soon as possible on Beechey Island and return to England. However, drifting ice from the polar pack filled the bay and surrounded the ships, preventing the *Breadalbane* from coming in beside the *North Star* and unloading. On Tuesday, August 9, the men of the *Breadalbane* worked their ship into the lee of Cape Riley's two-hundred meter bluffs across the bay from Beechey Island. Rigging up a system of blocks and tackles, they began to discharge their cargo, beginning with the coal. The next day, driven by the currents, ice began to pile up next to the ship. Fearing they would be crushed, the captain ordered the shorelines cast off, and the *Breadalbane* drifted seaward. With the *Phoenix* towing her, she took up a position about three kilometers to the west of Cape Riley.

By now, Fawckner and every other man on board the *Breadalbane* knew well the sound of ice pressing against the wooden hull. The curved wall of wood that ran from stem to stern amplified every sound. When struck, the wood reverberated, keeping the men from their sleep. They lay there, listening to the loud intermittent thunder. Occasionally there was a shriek as a larger piece pressed against the wales, the part of the ship just beneath the water. The sound most feared was the sound of something breaking, something giving way.

Eager to be out of the ice and heading back to England, the men filled sledges with bread and other provisions and hauled them across the broken ice to the *North Star*. Suddenly their attention was drawn back to their ship. Fawckner writes:

> "About ten a.m. the ice set upon the transport, giving her a nip which raised her about five feet, and did not 'ease' for about an hour. She did not suffer much by it. One piece of ice got under the keel, and kept her stern raised two feet until four p.m., when, by setting sail on the ship and heaving on ropes laid out on the ice (which was at the same time driving) the transport slipped off. We then ran up about a mile, and moored in a bight of the ice. The next day commenced discharging, working night and day, dragging the provisions on sledges to Beechey Island."

The ice continued to plague them. It was moving back and forth, driven by distant winds and currents. From the journal of Elisha Kent Kane, the famous American Arctic explorer, we know that on August 20, about eight hundred kilometers to the east of the *Breadalbane*, off the coast of Greenland, a strong gale was blowing. Inside his small brig, the *Advance*, Kane wrote:

> "By Saturday morning it blew a perfect hurricane. We had seen it coming, and were ready with three good hawsers out ahead,

and all things snug on board. Still it became heavier and heavier, and the ice began to drive more wildly than I thought I had ever seen it. I had just turned in to warm and dry myself during a momentary lull, and was stretching myself out in my bunk, when I heard the sharp twanging snap of a cord. Our six-inch hawser had parted, and we were swinging by the two others; the gale roaring like a lion to the southward."

The storm lasted two full days, dragging Kane's brig through the ice, parting hawsers, throwing ice up on the deck, driving the ship up the side of an iceberg, almost sinking it. Several times the *Advance* was almost crushed. The severity and duration of the storm suggest that it was part of a weather system that influenced the movement of ice around the *Breadalbane* in Barrow Strait.

In the middle of the storm, just after midnight on August 21, there was an ominous movement of the ice next to the *Breadalbane*. Fawckner wrote:

"The ice... to which we were secured started, obliging our moving east in tow of the *Phoenix*. I felt exceedingly uneasy in my bed, and got up; the ice was setting to the westward, and grating against the sides, but after rising, the thermometer then at 26 deg., I entertained no doubt of the ship's safety; and after moving about until three a.m. secured to the ice, midway between Beechey Island and Cape Riley, I again went to bed, but fortunately did not get in a sound sleep... About ten minutes past four, the ice passing the ship awoke me, and the door of my cabin, from the pressure, opened: I immediately hurriedly put on my clothes, and on getting up found some hands on the ice, endeavouring to save the boats, but they were instantly crushed to pieces; they little thought, when using their efforts to save the boats, that the ship was in so perilous a situation. I went forward to hail the *Phoenix*, for men to save the boats, and whilst doing so, the ropes by which we were secured parted, and a heavy nip took the ship making every timber in her creak, and the ship tremble all over. I looked in the main hold, and saw the beams giving way; I hailed those on the ice, and told them of our critical situation, they not for one moment suspecting it. I then rushed to my cabin, hauled out my portmanteau on the deck, and roared like a bull to those in their beds to jump out and save their lives. The startling effect on them might be more easily imagined than described. On reaching the deck those on the ice called out to me to jump over the side, that the ship was going over. I left my portmanteau and jumped over the side on the loose ice, and with difficulty and the assistance of those on the ice, succeeded in getting on the unbroken part, with the loss of the slippers I had on when quitting the vessel, with wet feet, etc.; the cold was little thought of at the exciting moment — life, not property, being the object to be saved. After being on the ice about five minutes, the timbers, etc., in the ship cracking up like matches would in the hand; it eased for a short time, and I with some others returned to the ship, with the view of saving some of our effects. Captain Inglefield now came running towards the ship. He ordered me to see if the ice was through the ship; and on looking down in the hold found all the beams, etc., falling about in a manner that would have been certain death to me had I ventured down there, but there was no occasion for that (I mean to ascertain the fact of the ice being through), it being too evident that the ship could not last many minutes; I then sounded the well, and found five feet in the hold, and whilst in the act of sounding, a heavier nip than before pressed out the starboard-bow, and the ice was forced right into the forecastle. Everyone then abandoned the ship, with what few clothes they saved — some with only what they had on; I merely saved a portmanteau, with a few things in it. The ship now began to sink fast, and from the time her bowsprit touched the ice, until her mastheads were out of sight, did not occupy above one minute and a half. It was a very sad and unceremonious way of being turned out of our ship. From the time the first nip took her, until her disappearance, did not occupy more than fifteen minutes.

I, as well as all the spectators of the last of the *Breadalbane*, was astonished at the rapid manner in which she went down. I could not have credited a ship sinking so fast, had she been laden with iron, or any other dead weight, whereas she was in ballast trim. My loss amounted to about One Hundred and Sixty or One Hundred and Seventy Pounds. I hope the Admiralty may repay me; but it is a very doubtful case. The loss to the Government amounted to about Seven Hundred Pounds.

This loss will hasten the *Phoenix's* departure, that being the only object (clearing the transport) she had in remaining so long. The shipwrecked crew, of course, are all anxious to get home; their pay ceases the day the vessel is lost."

Fawckner's next comment on the probable fate of Franklin's two ships, *Erebus* and *Terror*, was despairingly accurate:

"I can now easily imagine the way the two missing Arctic ships have never been heard of, and it is but too probable in my mind, they were lost not many miles from my old vessel, and that all hands met with a watery grave."

116

All twenty-one men on board the *Breadalbane* scrambled across the ice to the *Phoenix*. The ice that tore open the side of their ship allowed them to walk away unhurt. On August 24, the *Phoenix* carrying the crew of the *Breadalbane* and the survivors from M'Clure's ship, the *Investigator*, departed for England. Behind them, down in the blackness, streams of bubbles still issued from the drowned ship. Soon winter would arrive. With it would come an enormous stillness and the first season of the ice.

THE FINAL ATTEMPT

CHAPTER TWELVE

J uly, 1980. It was the year of Soviet tanks in Afghanistan, American hostages in Iran and the summer Olympics in Moscow. In July, as the athletes were returning home, we were putting together a final expedition to locate the *Breadalbane*.

It would be the last attempt. Funds had dried up. Supporters of the project were losing interest. If the ice-covered waters did not reveal their secret on this trip, it would be impossible to justify another search.

Early that summer I called Bill Graves, a senior editor at *National Geographic Magazine*.

"I'm sorry Joe," said Bill from his Washington office. "We won't be able to cover your travel expenses." I couldn't blame the *Geographic*. In 1978 the magazine had given me a one thousand dollar advance for first rights to the story. In 1979, thanks to Emory, the *Geographic* had paid half the cost of leasing the side-scan sonar. For two years in a row we had not found the ship.

An analysis of the two years showed that we had only been granted seven days of reasonable weather. Even when the sun was shining and the wind moderate, the search area was barricaded with ice which prevented us from running the classical, grid-like search pattern.

As in 1979, the only way we could afford another expedition was to keep it small. Only three of us would go; Emory, Gary and myself, with a minimum of equipment.

During the year we had kept in constant touch. When I told Emory about my conversation with Bill Graves, he laughed. "Not to worry," he said in his deep voice. "To be really successful, an expedition must rest on a firm foundation of financial insecurity."

A few weeks later I went down to Washington to talk to Emory in his office. On the fourth floor of the *National Geographic's* white marble tower on M Street, the office was crammed with film, packing cases and photographs. Emory, and his associate, Jim Stanfield, always seemed to be going somewhere. A map on the wall with pins stuck in it hinted that their photographic assignments had carried them all around the world. On Emory's desk was a small, hand-lettered sign: "When the going gets tough — lower your standards."

"Meet Al Chandler," said Emory, as a tall, white-haired man stepped into the office. "Al's the guy who builds the deep-sea camera systems. He's just put together something special for us." Emory moved over and pointed to a large photograph lying on his desk. The picture showed the new camera, dripping wet, coming out of a test pool. "It's small, light-weight and takes a picture every twenty seconds." Emory paused and looked up at me. "I'd like to take Al with us. If we could get a picture of the *Breadalbane*, it would change everything."

During the year I made several trips to Ottawa to inquire about the use of a Coast Guard ice-breaker. It was the most essential component of the expedition. In that cold and grey city, I met with Jim Clarke, the Director of Fleet Systems for the Canadian Coast Guard.

Clarke was built solidly with a wide, smiling face. The walls of his office were lined with photographs of ships in the Coast Guard's fleet. He sat at this desk toying with a yellow pencil. "The captain and crew of the *Labrador* feel pretty good about last summer's project," he said with a smile. "Everybody learned something. And everybody appreciated the film done by the CBC. I'd suggest you write directly to the Minister of Transport. Be very specific about what you want. Justify everything."

I wrote the letter, adding a revised technical proposal and a summary of the previous year's efforts. A month later I had a reply. If there was time, and if the ship was free of other duties, an ice-breaker would be available for three days' work at Beechey Island.

We were assigned the *John A. Macdonald*, one of the newest and biggest ice-breakers in the Coast Guard's fleet. Almost as long as a football field, she displaced over nine thousand tonnes. Her nine diesel-electric engines, housed deep in her steel metal interior, could drive her through the open sea at fifteen knots.

Late in March I flew to Boston to talk to Marty Klein. His side-scan sonar, and a technician to operate it, were essential to the expedition. However, the commercial lease rate was more than we could afford.

We met in the basement of John Hancock Hall. An hour earlier the upstairs auditorium had been filled with almost two thousand people watching an underwater film festival.

"Marty," I said, "I know you're always being approached for favours. But I..."

Marty held up the palm of his hand, urging me to stop. "I know what you're going to say. But I should tell you that we are in business to make money." He paused and tugged at his moustache. "We have a responsibility to our employees and shareholders. If we helped everybody with a shipwreck project, we'd be out of business in a month."

I knew that in spite of what he said, Marty, at heart, was a romantic.

His thoughts went beyond the balance sheet. Four years earlier he had used one of his side-scan sonars in a systematic search of Loch Ness. The monster was not found but, thanks to Marty and his equipment, a clear picture emerged of the steep-walled lake where it was supposed to dwell. An unusual formation of submerged, ring-shaped stones was called, in Marty's honour, Klein-Henge.

We had arranged to meet in the basement of John Hancock Hall because a party was being held after the film festival. The air in the large room was filled with laughter and the scent of whiskey and rum. One of the members of the party saw us talking and ambled over. I had met him somewhere, but couldn't recall his name. He was an older man, a physiologist in an eastern university. "Enjoyed what you told us tonight about the *Breadalbane*," he said, referring to my brief slide presentation. "Sure looks like the ice is a big problem." He looked at me and smiled. "If you were smart, you'd forget the Arctic and go back to doing what you do best — diving medicine."

After he left, Marty and I got up and started to head for the door. "How much money do you guys have this year?" he asked. I explained our financial position.

"Well, I've changed my mind," he said. "An Arctic shipwreck is really unusual and I like the way you keep on fighting. My Board of Directors may not like it, but once again you can count us in. Cover our costs and we'll give you Gary and the gear."

Money for the expedition began to trickle in. An anonymous donor in Toronto sent a cheque for one thousand dollars. Gordon Harrison of Dome Petroleum added two thousand more. After a lecture in Montreal, two young businessmen in the audience each sent five hundred dollar contributions. In early August I had a phone call from Nordair, the airline that flies passengers and freight into Canada's high eastern Arctic. "We've talked it over and would like to help out by giving you and your team reductions in the air fare between Montreal and Resolute Bay." On that same day, with Emory's help, I found a ship-positioning system that we could afford.

Telefix Canada is a small, high technology company operating out of a one-storey yellow brick building in Toronto. It is part of the sprawl of small businesses clustered in the northeast end of the city. Run by Don Davis, an easy-going young entrepreneur, Telefix provides light-weight equipment for field surveys. "Normally our systems are used by geologists and hydrographers," said Davis as we talked in his office. "An Arctic shipwreck is a new kind of problem."

I asked Davis how the equipment worked. He took a ballpoint pen and began sketching out the outline of Beechey Island and the curve of the nearby shore. "Basically our system is an electronic yardstick," he said. "A way of measuring the distance between the shore and the ice-breaker." He continued his sketch. "We put out two stations, about three kilometers apart on shore. The master station is located on the ice-breaker."

The telephone began to ring but Davis chose to ignore it. "The master station," he continued, "sends out a constant signal that is bounced off each shore station. The master station is really a small computer. By phase comparison it measures the signals coming in from each remote station. The ice-breaker's position is read out on a digital printer." The phone on the desk stopped ringing. "If you find the *Breadalbane*," he said confidently, "we'll plot its position to within one meter."

He stood up and offered his hand. "If your Foundation can cover our expenses, everything else is on us." He paused and looked down at the sketch he had made on his desk. "All you have to do is find the ship."

On August 11, I drove to Montreal to meet Emory, Gary and Al Chandler. The fourth addition to the team was Mike Moog, a technician from Telefix. An older man, Mike had spent part of his youth with the Royal Navy. At the last minute, two others who had paid their own expenses, joined us. Chris Matthews was a strong high school student with a keen interest in the Arctic. Maurice Haycock flew down from Ottawa.

"I want to be there when you find it," Maurice said. It was particularly important for Maurice to be with us. In a few weeks he would be celebrating his eightieth birthday.

Early the next morning, we were on Nordair's flight 504, bound for Resolute Bay. Five hours later, after stopping at Frobisher Bay, we flew over Barrow Strait. There was no sign of last year's ice.

At Resolute, the 737 landed heavily, sending up a spray of sand and gravel. We taxied in towards the small, green terminal. Parked next to it was a red and white helicopter belonging to the Coast Guard. Within the hour, all of us and our equipment were on board the *John A. Macdonald*.

By mid-afternoon of the next day, we had arrived at Beechey Island. A cold but gentle breeze blew in from the west. Except for a few scattered pans of ice, the water to the south of the island was open and clear.

Using the helicopter, it took Mike Moog about an hour to set up the shore stations for his positioning system. He landed on the foreshore of Beechey Island beneath the cliffs and then flew across the mouth of the bay to Cape Riddle. Both stations were set on a small tripod, their dish antennae pointing toward the search area.

While Mike was calibrating his shore stations, Gary set up his side-scan recording equipment on a table in a corner of the bridge. This time communication with the captain and the helmsman would be instant; if the tow-fish was too close to the sea floor or became caught in the ice, the men on the bridge could respond immediately.

As we worked on setting up our equipment, the captain of the *Macdonald* eyed us carefully. Steve Gomez was a big, barrel-chested man with beefy shoulders. "You boys sure know how to take over a bridge," he said. His voice was warm but authoritative. "That's okay. Just don't get any ideas about taking over my ship."

For a few moments he stood behind Gary, peering down at the complex equipment on the table. Then he looked out the windows that stretched the full length of the bridge. "Looks like you're in for better weather this year," he said, "the sea is only three-tenths covered with ice."

Men who make a living on the ice have a language all their own. If the ocean is completely covered, the condition is known as 10/10; half covered is 5/10. At 3/10 the ocean is almost free of ice. "Of course the tide may close things up a bit," he continued. "We'll see."

Just after seven o'clock I stepped out onto the wing of the bridge. The white railing was cold beneath my fingertips. The air was filled with the scent of snow and ice. The *Macdonald* moved slowly through the water, a small knot of seamen clustered at the stern preparing to launch the tow-fish. The sea was quiet, almost calm. As we struck the occasional ice floe, pushing it aside, a tremor ran along the keel of the ice-breaker.

At eight o'clock we began the search. The tow-fish was slipped over the side and lowered into the depths.

I stepped into the warmth of the bridge. Except for the hum of the electronic equipment and the occasional quiet order, it was silent.

"Keep your heading at one hundred degrees," said the captain.

In the far corner, Emory was busy setting up his camera and lights. "Nothing captures a moment like television," he had told me earlier in the day.

Emory's comment surprised me. He was one of the world's foremost still photographers. "Sure I take 35 mm stills. That's what I do best. But electronic imaging is going to take over. It's inevitable. Like steam engines replaced canvas sails." I watched Emory and Al unpack a broadcast-quality television camera and clean its lens.

Gary and Mike were sitting together hunched over the long table that held their equipment. Elbows on the table, Gary was peering through the steeple made by his fingers. The two men said nothing, each intent on the information flowing onto the paper and digital read-outs in front of them.

"Joe, I think you'd better take a look at this." Gary's voice was almost a whisper.

I held my breath and leaned forward. The recording pen fluttered steadily, tracing out a steep-walled trough that sliced into the sea floor. It was similar to the scours we had seen in 1978 and 1979. The trough was followed by another, this one curving, looking as if it had been made by a runaway plough.

"Damn, here we go again."

"What's our depth?"

"About ninety meters."

"There's another one!" It was Emory, who was leaning over the table. The light-weight television camera was cradled on his right-hand shoulder.

"Steady on course one hundred and ten."

The *Macdonald* was moving forward about two kilometers south of Beechey Island. Through the windows of the bridge I could see the sheer under-cliff and small waves breaking against the shore. Over my shoulder was Barrow Strait, flecked with ice floes that had retreated into the distance. Somewhere behind me the side-scan sonar followed the ship like a pilot fish trailing a whale.

The steady clicking of the position tracker seemed to get louder as we neared a depth of one hundred meters. The recorder pen moved swiftly. As a small outline began to appear on the paper, a hush fell across the bridge. Emory rapidly positioned his camera.

The outline moved down towards the centre of the recorder. Gary's eyes narrowed. He exhaled softly.

"That's it! I think that's it!"

"You're kidding."

"No, dammit. That's it! Look, there's her hull. I can't believe this! She's intact! Even her masts are still standing!"

"My God you're right!"

"Somebody note the co-ordinates!"

Six heads eagerly leaned in towards Gary's recorder. Trembling with excitement, we stared at the faint shadow of the *Breadalbane*. At last, after years of searching, we had found her, a pale ghost beneath the ice.

Gary's face was almost on top of the paper. His glasses had slipped down towards the tip of his nose.

"Will you look at that mother..."

"Sweet lady Jane!"

It was Emory. Despite his excitement, the television camera on his shoulder was as steady as a rock.

A muffled explosion came from beneath the bow of the *Macdonald*. In fitting tribute to our discovery, she had hit a big slab of ice and split it wide open.

CHAPTER THIRTEEN

We broke out the rum. The bar in the Officers' Mess was thrown open by Captain Gomez. A dozen glasses were suddenly on the table. For the next hour the smoke swirled around the scrabble of bodies and laughter. Gary was beaming. Emory held his glass high. "Vindicated," he boomed. "At long last we're vindicated."

The party lasted until four in the morning. Time after time we charged our glasses and toasted our fortunes. "Here's to our good luck with the weather," said Captain Gomez. "To the officers and crew of the *Macdonald*," shouted Mike. "To everyone who helped us," I added.

It was hard to believe that we had actually found it. The world's northernmost known shipwreck. In perfect condition. Most wooden ships that go down in shallow waters are reduced to a pile of rubble within months, smashed by waves and eaten by worms. Not this one. Thanks to freezing water and the ice, she was perfectly preserved. A time-capsule.

We spent the next day and a half taking more side-scan images of the sunken ship. A large red marker buoy was placed over the site and we steamed back and forth trailing the side-scan. Gary worked excitedly, directing the course of the ice-breaker. "We'll make a number of passes at different angles," he said. "That'll give us a composite view of the ship and the sea floor."

Using the position-fixing computer to verify our position, we made twelve separate passes over the *Breadalbane*. Each one gave us a different view.

The two masts were clearly etched on the recorder print-out paper. The ship was sitting on the sea floor, her masts tilted over on a slight angle. The tip of her bowsprit was broken off. The third mast seemed to have fallen clear of the ship and was lying on the sea floor.

About a hundred meters from the hull, etched in the sediments, was a deep ice scour. Both masts were surrounded by thick material hinting of yards and, when the imagination took wing, furled canvas sails.

Emory and I ran down to the *Macdonald's* radio room and sent telegrams to some of the people who had supported the expedition. We made a ship-to-satellite call to the news bureau at *National Geographic*. "I'll have a photograph of the side-scan image down to you as soon as I can," Emory promised Bob Radcliff in Washington. "In the meantime, let's work together on a press release."

A few days later, the release went out. It was titled: "SONAR FINDS GHOST SHIP SUNK IN CANADIAN ARCTIC." Four pages long, the release described the *Breadalbane* and her role in Arctic maritime history. With it was the side-scan sonar image that would end up on the front page of hundreds of newspapers around the world.

Our next step was to try and take a photograph of the *Breadalbane*. A picture of the deck or hull would contain vital information about the condition of the wood and its covering of century-old marine growth.

A small, flat-bottomed aluminium boat manned by three of the *Macdonald's* crew, was lowered over the side. Landing gently on the surface of the sea, we motored away, steering around the small pans of ice drifting with the tide. The ocean was calm, almost oily.

In the centre of the boat Emory and Al had piled a coil of black rubber cable and, on top of it, the underwater camera. The camera, a pair of lights and a television camera were attached to a T-shaped aluminium frame. The television camera was our seeing eye and would help us avoid getting tangled in the wreck.

Our small boat, with its battered sides, approached the marker buoy and slowed down. Gary uncoiled a thin white nylon line and fastened a small grappling hook to one end. "Going fishing," he said and hefted it over the side.

"That's pretty sophisticated technology you're using," said Emory with a smile.

"It may be medieval my friend, but it works."

A hundred meters below us, the grappling hook hit the bottom and bounced along on the sediments, drawn by the drift of our boat. Gary held the line lightly with his fingertips.

"That's it. We've got her."

The white nylon line went tight. The boat stopped. "The anchor feels like it's hooked into the wood of the hull. Give me a hand making it tight."

We hauled in on the line until it was bowstring tight, running straight down into the blackness beneath us.

I glanced at the sky. The sun had slipped in behind a layer of cloud. Around us, pushed by the increasing tide, was an incoming clutter of sea-ice. Some of the white pans were bigger than our boat. In the background, Beechey's dark cliffs glared across the water.

We lifted the aluminium frame with its cameras and attached it to the nylon line. Working over the stern of the boat, Emory and Al positioned the frame so that it would run down unhindered toward the ship.

"Lower away." Hand over hand, we payed out the black rubber cable over the stern of the boat. The cameras descended under a stream of small bubbles. All eyes turned to the television screen. Emory leaned over and wrapped his thick fingers around the nylon line. "That sucker is as hard as a mother-in-law's heart."

Without warning there was a sharp noise, as if someone had stepped on a light-bulb. A puff of blue smoke crept out of the television monitor.

Pulling a screwdriver from his pocket, Al opened the back of the television set. "We've burned out a condenser," he said.

"Forget it Al. We'll shoot it blind," said Emory. His voice was on edge. "Lower away."

It was not an easy decision. Emory's aluminium frame held cameras and lights worth tens of thousands of dollars. Without the television to steer us, they might get snared in the *Breadalbane's* rigging.

As we struggled with the heavy weight of the cameras and cable, trying to lower it smoothly, the ice moved in. Borne on the tide, it came at us slowly, inexorably. Within minutes we were surrounded by a gang of pans. They hissed and bristled, banging against us. For a while we fought them with pike-poles, pushing their white flanks away from the cable which hung over the stern.

Somewhere far below, the camera was taking pictures automatically.

Finally, Emory held both hands in the air. "That's it. We're surrounded. Let's not be like Custer. Let's get out of here."

We hauled up the cameras. The cable came up over the side dripping, splashing on our arms and legs. The water stung with cold. One of the seamen tied a large red marker buoy to the end of the nylon line. He released it and we drifted free.

It took almost half an hour to work our way back through the ice toward the dark red hull of the *Macdonald*. A slash of pink scarphed its way across the western sky. Blocks and tackle were lowered from the big ship and attached to our bow and stern. By the time we were lifted clear of the ocean and reached the deck, a river of ice had swept over the shipwreck area. We looked closely, searching. Severed from its line, the marker buoy was gone.

That night a message came into the *Macdonald's* radio room requesting Captain Gomez to return his ship to Resolute Bay. A small tanker needed assistance through the eastern section of Barrow Strait.

Fortunately, the request did not take effect immediately; we had one more day.

That night the weather changed. The wind came up out of the east steady and strong, gusting to twenty knots. The ice had vanished. The sea over the *Breadalbane* was covered with whitecaps.

We waited until noon to launch our small boat. A knot of men, their collars up, their hands jammed into their pockets, came down to watch us load our gear. Hydraulic motors hummed and we were picked up and slung over the side by the davits. Just then Captain Gomez came down off the bridge.

"Good luck boys. I'll try to keep the ship upwind to give you some protection from the waves."

The blocks over our heads creaked and, in a measured way, we were lowered down to the sea. As soon as we touched the surface, the small boat began to roll.

We motored across the writhing greyness. Waves broke all around us, their white foaming tops falling into steep troughs. Welcome back to the old Widow-Maker, I thought.

Within minutes, despite the rolling of the boat, Gary had hooked into the side of the *Breadalbane*.

"Gotcha," he shouted, his voice like a steam calliope.

We rushed to the stern and pulled the line in tight.

The wind picked up. The boat pitched and rolled over on a big swell and then settled into a trough. A glistening wave creamed in over the stern and into the scuppers.

We uncoiled the cable and lowered the cameras. After we had been lowering for almost ten minutes, Al looked up and shook his head.

"Damn," he said, his voice on edge. "We've run out of cable."

Except for a blur of suspended particles, the television screen was empty.

"The current must be pushing against the cable, moving it away from the ship."

All eyes were on the screen. It was filled with swirling motes of life, drifting hordes of plankton. Then, as we watched, an object emerged out of the darkness. It was hard and long, wooden, a section of the ship's railing.

Everyone pushed in closer to the television. The wooden railing in front of us was broken at one end and covered with sea growth. Even the grain of the wood was clearly visible. No one spoke. This was the first time in one hundred and twenty-seven years that human eyes had seen the *Breadalbane*.

Emory's face was mottled with excitement. "Look at the condition of the wood!"

Gary, his eyes wide, was kneeling in front of the screen. He stood up, so slowly and smoothly, that he might have been underwater. He shoved one fist high in the air. "Unbelievable. She's a beauty and she's ours."

"Lift the camera one meter."

The dark waters flared white as Emory's strobe-light went off. At each firing, a small section of ship blazed with colour. We forgot the wind and the waves. We forgot the *Macdonald*. For the next half hour the centre of our existence was the flickering screen.

A wave larger than the rest lifted the boat and dropped it sharply into a trough. Once again a wall of grey water splashed over the stern. The boat pitched and trembled.

Under Emory's direction the camera was lowered for close-ups and then lifted for wide-area photographs. Each flash of the strobe-light exposed a blush of sea-growth on wood.

Another large wave struck the stern and raced across the deck. One of the seamen, a young man with a towel around his neck for a scarf, shot me a glance.

Al wiped freezing beads of water from his cheek and looked up at the sky. It was the colour of lead. "What do you think Joe?" The wind snatched the words from his mouth.

"It's time to go," I answered.

"While we're still afloat," added Gary.

That night, as the ship steamed back towards Resolute Bay, we gathered in the officers' lounge to celebrate Maurice Haycock's eight-ieth birthday. It was fitting that he, who had so much to do with the early days of the search, should have been with us.

"I really don't deserve this," he said, his old face beaming.

Two hours later, after repeated excursions to the table where drinks had been set out, we sat down to watch the eleven o'clock news. Since 1973 the CBC had been beaming a television signal from the Anik satellite into the high Arctic. Earlier that day, Bob Radcliff from the *National Geographic* had called to say that news of our discovery had been picked up by the wire services and would be broadcast by the CBC at eleven o'clock. Warmed by our achievement, drinks in hand, we settled down to watch the show.

The screen filled with images of an old ship. We watched in stunned silence as the announcer described a sinking many years earlier. There were multiple close-up views of her deck and the ice around her hull. These were followed by intimate views of her cabin structure and old newspaper clippings with banner headlines telling the world about her sinking. In four thousand meters of water off the south coast of New-foundland, seventy years after she had been holed by the ice, the *Titanic* had been found.

CHAPTER FOURTEEN

A few days later we returned to southern Canada. Gary's side-scan picture of the *Breadalbane* showing her hull and two masts was released by the *National Geographic* and was picked up by wire services everywhere.

SHIPWRECK PRESERVED IN ARCTIC ICE
SAILING SHIP IS FOUND IN NORTHWEST PASSAGE
FROZEN TIME CAPSULE DISCOVERED!
ARCTIC SHIP INTACT
1853 SAILING VESSEL FOUND IN CANADIAN ARCTIC
SUNKEN SHIP FOUND IN THE ICY DEEP

From Germany to Australia, newspapers showed the ice ship lying ghost-like on the sea floor beneath the ice. The CBC used the same image and some of Emory's video tape, as part of a long segment for the national news. The dean of broadcasters, Walter Cronkite, announced the discovery on the six o'clock CBS news.

Shortly afterwards we found out that, despite the claim, the *Titanic* had not been found after all. Jack Grimm, a Texas millionaire, had spent hundreds of thousands of dollars searching the Atlantic south of Newfoundland. Desperate for publicity to keep his venture going another year, he and the William Morris Agency had released news of their "find." It didn't seem to matter that they had no proof. The news media, with its voracious appetite, had swallowed it whole.

The weeks that followed were filled with phone calls and thank you letters to all the people who had assisted the expedition. Telegrams of congratulations poured in, including one from Pierre Elliott Trudeau, the Prime Minister of Canada.

Emory's photographs of the ship were developed in Toronto. They showed sections of the foredeck and the foremast. Through a fine mist of plankton, we could see the starboard railing and a capstan. Close-up views showed anemones and brittle stars clinging to the wreck. The wooden planks of the deck, smooth and straight, were in perfect condition.

Finding the *Breadalbane* changed my life. For years I had been trying to increase human awareness of the underwater world. Since 1970, I had been concentrating my efforts on the Arctic. As a diving physician, my primary concern was safe and efficient diving. However, another interest was to get more people to respect the sea and its hidden universe of animals and plants.

The *Breadalbane* was an opportunity to bring all these elements together. Using the ship as a focal point, it would be possible to design a series of dives using the most advanced diving systems available. We could study the ship and photograph it. We could also study the marine life attached to its surface and the sea-ice floating over its masts.

The best time for such a project was in the spring. In April and May, the Arctic Ocean was frozen solid and a fathom thick. We could build a camp on the ice. Holes could be cut through the ice to allow divers to descend to the wreck. A string of lights could be hung down to light the entire ship.

I called Emory in Washington. Sensing a new technical challenge, he was passionately enthusiastic.

"We'll use 747 landing lights," he said. "A string of them. Each one puts out six hundred thousand candle power. With a big generator, we could hang forty of them like chandeliers along the length of the ship."

"I want the ultimate underwater photograph," Emory continued, his voice rising. "It will show the entire ship, from bow to stern. It will be everybody's dream image of a shipwreck, a three-page foldout for the magazine. I want a picture that will retire all the awards for underwater photography."

He paused on the other end of the phone.

"But what about the ice?" he asked. "How do you know it won't be moving?"

"I don't," I said. "But the ship is only about two kilometers from the island. There's a good chance the ice over it will be solid all the way to the shore."

In April the visibility underwater would be perfect, the water so clear that we could see more than the length of the ship. With luck, Emory might get his picture. However, he would need to build the lighting system from scratch. And the ice, always unpredictable, would have to co-operate.

No one knew more about the technical side of Arctic diving than Phil Nuytten. Since 1972, when he and his divers joined my Arctic III expedition, his company had logged more than two thousand Arctic dives. Most of them had been made in the Beaufort Sea for Dome Petroleum. I called Phil and outlined my plans for the spring expedition.

"Dropping down to the *Breadalbane* would be one hell of a challenge," he said. "We could approach it using three of our underwater systems — a diving bell, our small submarine or the WASP suit."

Essentially the WASP suit is a submarine that you wear. It is a one-man tethered submersible that weighs less than 3000 kilograms above the surface. The pilot looks out through an acrylic dome and operates two anthropomorphic arms. He motors about using six small thrusters, hovering in the water like a helicopter. The WASP contains a complex life-support system and can take a diver to 700 meters without getting him cold or wet, nor exposing to him to pressure and the bends. The suit was one of the most important recent inventions in deep diving.

A picture began to form in my mind. The *Breadalbane* sitting on the sea floor with a diving bell hanging just above the deck-house. Two men inside the diving bell, preparing to swim out. Hovering in the background, a small three-man submarine, *Sea-otter*. Off to the side, approaching slowly, a man in a WASP suit.

More than anything, a major expedition to the *Breadalbane* needed a good science programme. It would be essential to study not only the ship, but the sediments that surrounded it, the marine life attached to it, and the sea-ice that floated over its masts. To direct the science programme, I turned to Steve Blasco, the marine geologist I had met at the North Pole. I phoned him at his laboratory at the Bedford Institute in Halifax.

"Sure I'd like to get involved," he said, "but I'm heavily committed. We're really busy in the Beaufort Sea. Let me look at my schedule."

Less than a week later Steve called back to say that he would join the team.

Steve was specifically interested in the ice scour near the ship. "We've never had a chance to study one up close. By packing the submarine with instruments and getting an intimate look through a view-port, we could learn a lot."

It was easy finding other scientists who wanted to join the expedition. Dr. Roger Pilkington was a sea-ice specialist working with Dome Petroleum in Calgary. In 1978, Roger and I had worked together diving and filming ice pressure ridges in the Beaufort Sea. For years Roger had been trying to get close-up views of submerged ice. "Most of our information has come indirectly," he said, "with lowered instruments. It will be a splendid opportunity to dive down and use the best of all instruments, the human eye."

Roger's colleague, marine biologist, Rick Hoos, felt the same way. Between 1970 and 1976, Rick had logged more than fifty dives in a small submersible studying marine life in the cold waters of British Columbia. "There's no substitute," he said. "The only way to study the sea is to go down into it. Count me in. It's a part of the ocean that no one has seen."

As we talked, Rick passed along some information that proved invaluable.

"I'll bet your ship is pretty well covered with sea life. There've been more than a hundred years for colonies to establish themselves. At that depth they'll probably be mostly animals. They'll be attached to the exposed surfaces — the hull, the deck and the masts — the interior should be pretty clean."

I didn't have far to go to find an archaeologist interested in the *Breadalbane*. Dr. Walter Kenyon, a senior archaeologist at the Royal Ontario Museum, had been delighting history students at the University of Toronto for many years. As a pre-medical student, I had been one of them. A consummate scholar, with a flair for wit and irreverence, he had a special passion for the Arctic.

Kenyon was the kind of professor who, when he could, "lived" his history. He had camped on the small island in James Bay where Thomas James had "sunk" his ship to save it from the ice. He had spent two summers leading expeditions to Kodlunarn Island where Frobisher had mined for "gold." No stranger to long weeks in the field, Kenyon kept cold and hardship at bay with an ample supply of good spirits.

"Exciting project," he said to me as we sat in his office drinking coffee. "Few things bring history more alive than a shipwreck. When do we begin?"

I explained my plan. "It should take about two weeks to put together the campsite. Everything will be flown to Resolute Bay and then hauled across the ice by Cat train. We'll make a small landing strip on the ice and fly back and forth to Resolute by Twin Otter."

"I wish I were a lot younger," grumbled Kenyon. "I'd like to dive down there myself."

"We'll try to let you have a quick dive in the diving bell, just for a..."

"Not me you don't." Coffee ran over the side of his cup as he quickly lowered it to the table.

"But Walter," I laughed, "we'll keep it unpressurized. Sitting in the diving bell will be like sitting in an elevator."

"Really?"

"Sure. Phil and his divers can lower you down fifty meters or so. With the big lights on, you'll see everything and you won't get wet."

"Well...maybe. Give me some time to think about it." He arched an eyebrow. "But tell me, how are your divers going to get down to the wreck? I mean right on it."

Kenyon was familiar with SCUBA diving. In the 1960s, he and his associates had done some classical shallow diving in the French River for fur trade artifacts — pots, pans, axes. However, it was at depths considerably less than where the *Breadalbane* lay.

"Our time on the bottom will be severely restricted," I answered. "To spend thirty minutes on the ship will require four hours of decompression. The divers will have to breathe a mixture of oxygen and helium."

"You won't be able to do much archaeology," he said.

"I know. It's just too deep. As far as archaeology is concerned, we'll be limited to taking photographs and, if possible, recovering easily accessible things from the deck or the deck-house."

Walter suggested that we contact Dr. Charles Hett at the Canadian Conservation Institute in Ottawa. "He's a good conservator," said Walter. He knows how to preserve objects drowned for a long time in the sea."

I added Hett's name to the growing list of people who were interested in the project. Also on the list was Dr. Alan McGowan, head of the Ship Division at the National Maritime Museum in Greenwich, England. Alan had been recommended by several people as one of the world's experts on nineteenth century sailing ships.

In the midst of this ground swell of enthusiasm for the next *Breadalbane* expedition, I ran into something I should have anticipated. The impassive force of bureaucracy. It started with a phone call from the Prince of Wales Heritage Centre in Yellowknife: The voice was flat and perfunctory. It offered no congratulations for the discovery of the *Breadalbane* nor did it have any suggestions for what might be done in the future. Instead it merely asked one question.

"Did you have a permit to search for the *Breadalbane*?"

137

CHAPTER FIFTEEN

I was thunderstruck. Since 1970, when we first began our Arctic expeditions, no one had ever suggested the need for a permit.

But this was different. This was a shipwreck that had suddenly received world-wide attention. In the bureaucratic mind it evoked images of historical treasures and plundering divers.

It took a moment to regain my composure. Then I became annoyed. All we had done was to find and photograph a shipwreck. Without any help from the Prince of Wales Heritage Centre — or any other institution for that matter. The question was repeated. "Did you have a permit?"

"We weren't diving on the ship," I said, my temper rising. "We were only taking pictures."

I should have stopped there, but I didn't. The years of effort and frustration drove me forward. "Guys like you give me a pain," I said. "You always call when the work is done. You don't ask if you can help. Oh no. All you're interested in is if the bloody forms are filled out."

Gradually the individual who called realized that it was futile to press his point. We were not diving and not engaged in archaeology. There was really no need for a permit at this stage. We were simply searching and taking pictures.

But I had done the wrong thing. Unwittingly I had tangled with the world of memoranda and committee meetings. I was setting in motion a monolith, as implacable as a field of moving ice. Like all things of bureaucratic origin, it would evolve slowly. It would gather its strength out of distant committee rooms populated by experts who knew nothing of the ocean's depths or diving. A few months later it would try again, in its own amorphous way, to scuttle the expedition.

During the last months of 1980, I travelled across Canada pulling together the various elements of the final expedition. I checked over everything, including applying for an archaeological permit. I sent an outline of the work we planned to do to the Interdepartmental Committee on Archaeology in Yellowknife. Without their approval, we could

139

not remove anything from the ship. This was somewhat ironical since we did not plan to do any marine archaeology. The *Breadalbane* was too deep. All we hoped to do was make a detailed photographic assessment. If an object such as the ship's wheel or compass was readily accessible, we hoped to bring it back for museum display.

As always, the hardest part was the money. The size of the camp and the number of weeks it would have to operate meant that we needed more than' three hundred thousand dollars.

Fortunately, there were a number of Canadians who felt there was a big stake in the future of the Northwest Passage. For these people, scientific understanding and practical experience under the ice of Lancaster Sound was an important step. It would assist in the wiser use of Canada's northern ocean. It would fill in gaps in our knowledge. And indirectly, it would help in the search for Arctic offshore resources. The money began to come in.

In Montreal, Fed-Nav, a shipping company with Arctic interests, came forward with twenty thousand dollars. In Calgary, Dome Petroleum sent a cheque for fifty thousand dollars. In Toronto, the Donner Foundation, an institute that had been supporting Arctic research for many years, made a magnificent offer of one hundred and fifty thousand dollars. For once it looked as if one of my Arctic research programmes would be sufficiently funded.

Non-cash contributions would eventually add up to more than seven hundred thousand dollars. These came in various ways. Each scientist found support from his own institution. George Hobson at Polar Shelf offered to provide the essential elements of the ice-camp: insulated dwellings, stoves, radios, generators and the dozens of items needed to support a team of twenty-five men on the ice for over a month. The Department of National Defence, whose assistance had been so vital to our expeditions since 1970, tentatively agreed to fly all our diving gear, some thirty tonnes, from southern Canada to Resolute Bay.

Once our equipment was in Resolute, we still had to transport it across Cornwallis Island and then over the ice of Wellington Channel to Beechey Island. It would be an arduous journey over the ice. In Resolute I talked to Tom Wallace who ran a construction and supply company. For six years Tom and his wife had been living in Resolute running a camp and providing heavy equipment and other facilities for northern exploration companies. Tom had a D-8 Caterpillar that he would hook up to sleds to make a Cat train. I hoped to use this to haul our camp and equipment from Resolute to the site.

He was enthusiastic. "We've got two sleds that will haul a lot of the heavy stuff," he told me. "The lighter things like tents, food and so on can be flown into a small airstrip we'll make on the ice next to the camp."

Tom knew the Arctic intimately. He had seen its winter storms and felt its crushing cold. He was hesitant about only one thing — driving the Cat train across Wellington Channel. "It depends on the ice," he said. "If we have a good cold winter then the ice should be thick enough to support the Cat train. If not, we've got a serious problem."

By the last week in February everything was ready to go. Phil's diving systems were being crated for shipping. Emory's underwater lighting system was in the last stages of construction. The scientists were packing their gear and Tom was oiling up his D-8 Cat.

Then I got the phone call.

It came from Resolute Bay, late one afternoon, via satellite. Some weeks earlier I had spoken to Ed Lewis, an engineer at the Canada Centre for Inland Waters. For years, Ed and his colleagues had been carrying out physical oceanography studies in Barrow Strait near Resolute. I asked Ed if he would take the time to fly over to Beechey Island to look at the ice over the *Breadalbane*. How thick was it? Was it broken up or flat?

Ed responded in the manner so typical of those who work in the high Arctic. "Sure I'll do it," he said. "Glad to help out." He also offered to measure the currents close to the sea floor. Information about the currents was vital to the success of the diving programme. If the currents were too strong they could affect the safety and efficiency of divers working on the ship.

Over the phone Ed's voice was barely audible. "I hate to be the one to tell you this," he said, "but the ice over the *Breadalbane* is in pretty rough shape." There was a long pause. The phone connection, linked through thousands of kilometers of space, went silent.

"Would you like to speak up a little Ed," I said. "I can hardly hear you."

"I said the ice south of Beechey Island is in pretty rough shape."

"Damn."

"We flew over there in a helicopter, set up camp and stayed for a day. The ice is solid but broken up. In some places it's pretty thin. It's badly rafted and hummocked. At eye level it looks like a miniature mountain range."

I closed my eyes. A picture of up-ended blocks, wildly angled and jutting into the sky, came into view. I waited for what Ed would say next.

"The good news is that there is not much current near the bottom. Less than a quarter of a knot. Your big chandelier lights should hang straight down."

"That's great," I said. "But tell me more about the ice. What about building an ice-camp?"

There was another long pause. "Pretty risky Joe," he said. "You might be able to build it over the ship, but I doubt it. There's no telling about the ice." The phone seemed to go dead.

"I guess I'd better get up there and see for myself."

Later I flew north to Resolute with a vivid image of Ed's description suspended in my mind. At Polar Shelf's camp, I climbed into a helicopter and flew east. Climbing to one thousand meters, we followed the south coast of Cornwallis Island.

As we sped across Wellington Channel, I began to wonder what Ed had been talking about. The sea-ice below the helicopter was as smooth as a billiard table. Then, about halfway across, I saw the first big pressure ridge. It ran from north to south, a twisting white line, a column of up-ended blocks pushed together by enormous forces.

It was followed by another and then another, a series of low-lying walls that merged and crossed each other on the way out to the horizon. Near Beechey Island, they joined to become a network, an endless series of ramparts that would take days, perhaps weeks, for the Cat train to penetrate.

We landed on the ice near the *Breadalbane*. The temperature was minus fifteen degrees Celsius. Fortunately there was no wind. As far as the eye could see, it looked like the ice had exploded from below. Row after row of tortured and mangled blocks ran out into Barrow Strait and back towards Beechey's sheer cliffs.

I remembered something I had seen several years earlier. It was in another part of the Northwest Passage, about a hundred kilometers southwest of Resolute Bay. The sea-ice where we had landed the Twin Otter had been two meters thick, but suddenly out in front of us was a black hole some five meters wide. I had peered over the edge into the calm black water. The hole, already freezing in at the edges, was made by a D-8 Cat that had driven over a crack and plunged through. It had fallen more than one hundred meters to the bottom. Inside the cab of the Cat, trapped by a jammed door, was the unbreathing body of the driver.

I simply couldn't take a chance on jeopardizing the lives of any of my men.

Cursing, I kicked at the ice and tried to compose what I would say to all those people — the sponsors, supporters and team members — who had prepared for this expedition for almost a year.

The snow crunched underfoot. Somewhere below me was the ship, its two masts standing tall in the current.

I later found out that at approximately the same time as I was walking back through the white silence to the waiting helicopter, a letter arrived at my desk in Toronto. It was from Yellowknife, more specifically, from the "Interdepartmental Committee on Archaeology representing the Federal and Territorial agencies that are responsible for archaeological protection and research in the Northwest Territories." The Committee had decided that it was "unable to licence the archaeological aspect of the project..." Bureaucracy, the human equivalent of the ice, was hard at work.

ON BOARD THE BREADALBANE

CHAPTER SIXTEEN

F our thousand kilometers south of the Northwest Passage, where the arm of Cape Cod begins to reach out from the mainland into the Atlantic, lies the small town of Falmouth, Massachusetts. During the summer its tree-shadowed streets are crowded with tourists. In winter, when the same streets are filled with snow blowing in from the Atlantic, it is a good place to think and to study. For some people, like Chris Nicholson, it is also a splendid place to invent things.

Although he holds no university degree, Chris Nicholson looks like a scholar. He peers at the world with owl-like eyes behind thick-lensed glasses. Whether in his office or on the deck of a ship, Chris moves hesitantly, as if his mind is on other things.

Chris Nicholson was born in a small town in southern Indiana. He grew up in a world that centred around the annual high school science fair. Between 1968 and 1972 Chris won ten major awards for his innovative projects, which included a solar furnace, a sonar system and, in his last two years of high school, a pair of small, remotely-controlled underwater vehicles.

These vehicles became his passion. Ever since he was a small boy, there was something inside Chris Nicholson steering him towards the sea. He read every book, fact or fiction, on the subject. When his schoolmates were out playing baseball, Chris was reading *Run Silent, Run Deep*. For him, the best days of his teenage life were spent alone in a room filled with machine tools, workship manuals, Plexiglass hemispheres and silicone chips. Chris wanted to build things that would take human beings into the ocean without getting wet.

In 1972, Chris graduated from high school and travelled south to New Orleans to be closer to the sea. Soon he was designing and building underwater equipment, including television systems, for Michelle LeClaire, a small diving company. By the end of the decade he was working in Holland for a Dutch company that had a big investment in offshore oil. He and his associates were responsible for building a remote underwater vehicle that weighed two thousand kilograms, moved through the water with three hundred and fifty kilograms of thrust, and carried a two hundred and seventy kilogram payload.

In January of 1981, Chris came back to the United States and began living in Falmouth. He had worked out a professional arrangement with a small oceanographic company called Benthos Incorporated. For twenty years, Benthos had been building sophisticated undersea systems, including deep-sea cameras and communications equipment that had gone to the farthest ocean depths. Benthos wanted to build a remotely piloted vehicle. Chris Nicholson wanted a company to help him with new ideas he had for a small light-weight system. A deal was struck.

In spite of the accord there was one small problem. The Board of Directors insisted that the vehicle must be built and tested within four months.

Chris felt that he could do it. He knew that his invention was something special. His vehicle was not the first of its kind but it had a number of unique features. It was small, compact and exquisitely instrumented. Its force-balanced thrusters would allow pin-point positioning hundreds of meters down, by an operator sitting on the deck of a ship. It would have a control box that fitted into the palm of a hand. It would dive to a depth of six hundred meters and travel to the end of its tether at a speed of three knots. Initially its payload would be cameras and lights.

Deep ocean cameras were a technical area where Benthos had more experience than any other company. They had recently built a thirty-five millimeter camera that took four hundred exposures, and was linked to a strobe-light. Incredibly, it weighed less than half a kilogram in water.

Beginning in January, Chris worked on the problem for twelve hours a day, seven days a week. Lack of time and sleep, and his obsession with doing things right, strained the fabric of his life. His personal relationships, his marriage and even his health were threatened. But by the end of April, he had finished the job.

It was Emory who first told me about Chris Nicholson's invention. As he talked, I knew he was describing a way of minimizing the problem of the ice and stealing a look at the *Breadalbane*.

"It's a marvelous camera platform," he said. "We could make a series of images along the deck and hull that would give us a much better idea of the condition of the ship. Nicholson's system is no bigger than a coffee table and it flies with the precision of a helicopter. We could hover it over the masts and run it along the length of the hull. With luck we might even be able to look inside."

I listened, responding to his enthusiasm.

"The television pictures would let us see where we are at all times. When we spot something interesting — pow — we zap it with the colour camera."

By postponing the big expedition, we had lost precious momentum. A big project like this one could slip easily from people's minds. Putting the remotely piloted vehicle down on the *Breadalbane* would help to regain some of that momentum. It would also allow us to "map" sections of the wreck and make better use of our time when we finally dove down to the deck.

I flew down to Falmouth and saw the vehicle perform in the Benthos test pool. It responded flawlessly to every command. After a few minutes practice I even operated it myself.

Before I went home I decided to sign a contract to lease the vehicle for a reconnaissance of the *Breadalbane*. Preparations were made throughout the summer and by late August we were ready to go.

In the morning of the 1st of September, we lifted off from Montreal's Dorval Airport and flew north over the great pine forests of Quebec. By about 11:30 we were high over the spruce bogs and pre-Cambrian granite of the northern part of the province. A few kilometers ahead, blue and serene, was Hudson Strait, the wide waterway that connected the Labrador Sea to Hudson Bay.

Bounded on the north by Baffin Island and on the south by the province of Quebec, Hudson Strait had beckoned and ruined the fortunes of many of the early explorers. So open, so wide, it promised a great expanse of ocean to the west and a passage to distant Cathay. For almost two centuries, beginning in 1610, men like Hudson, James and Foxe had sailed their small cockleshell boats through its treacherous reefs and currents, pushing west until they were trapped by the ice or the sandy sloping shoulders of the far shore. For all these men, particularly Henry Hudson who was set adrift by a mutinous crew, Hudson Strait was a steep-walled river of illusion.

Sur.ounding me in the aircraft, reading and talking, were the twelve other members of this year's expedition. Things were running smoothly. Two thousand kilometers ahead of us, stacked up in neat piles in the airport at Resolute, was four thousand kilograms of equipment including the remotely piloted vehicle and all its cameras. Sent up ahead a week earlier, it had been received and organized by George Hobson's men of Polar Shelf. A few kilometers south of the equipment, anchored at the mouth of the Bay, was the Canadian Coast Guard ice-breaker, *Pierre Radisson*. Its crew and captain were awaiting our arrival.

The seats around me were filled with old and new faces. Across the aisle was Chris Nicholson, reading a technical manual and making notes. Sitting beside him were Ron Church, Gary Hayward and Mike

Knight, the support team from Benthos. Ron Church personified the enthusiasm that this expedition had generated. Ron had set aside his role of President of the company to don blue jeans and come north to help out.

Sitting behind me were Bill Mason and Allan Gelhard from the National Film Board and George James from the CBC's *Fifth Estate*. Beside them were Peter Zimolong, a positioning expert from Telefix Canada. Directly in front of me, deep in conversation, were Emory Kristof, Al Chandler and Joe Schershel, all from *National Geographic*. Finally, several rows back, sitting alone, was Phil Nuytten, reading a book on Kwakiutl totem pole carving.

So far, this fourth trip to the *Breadalbane* had been flawless. Nordair, the airline of the eastern Arctic, had given us a generous discount on tickets and freight. Canadian Customs, usually a formidable barrier against bringing American underwater cameras across the border, had permitted us to bring over $400,000 worth of one-of-a-kind equipment under a temporary permit. Pleased with the results of last year's work, the Coast Guard had allowed us, for a few days, the use of the *Pierre Radisson*. She and her sister ship, the *Sir John Franklin*, were the most modern and efficient government ice-breakers operating in Canadian Arctic waters.

I gazed out the window at an enormous iceberg drifting west on the pale blue waters of the Strait. It was alone on the sea, its twin spires rearing one hundred meters up from its wide sway-backed body. The iceberg was a wanderer calved many months ago in the northern reaches of Baffin Bay. In the seasons that separated its birth from today, it had drifted south along the indented coast of Baffin Island and then turned west.

The jet-stream silence was broken by the crackle of the intercom. "Ladies and gentlemen," said the laconic voice, "this is your captain speaking. Unfortunately we are going to have to turn back. Frobisher Bay is fogged in and we are unable to land."

The 737 lifted its silver wing and banked slowly to the right. I looked backwards to see the blue of Hudson Strait disappear into the haze. Under a clear and cloudless sky, we headed south.

At five o'clock that night we were back in Montreal. A September rain sleeted across the streets and hinted of the coming of winter. After checking into a motel near the airport, we shuffled into the bar.

"Impressive beginning," came a smoky voice from the end of the table. Silence. "A truly stirring adventure." The laughter was weak. I said very little, letting the conversation follow its own channels. On the way back down south, we had stopped in Fort Chimo. I had been told by a scowling attendant that most of our gear, two full pallet-loads, had not arrived in Resolute but was sitting inside a shed in Frobisher Bay. I would have to wait until morning to be sure. We had one of those silent, two-drink nights and everybody went to bed early.

We did not get airborne again until the next night at ten o'clock. Six hours later, after making a stop in Frobisher Bay, we landed dog-tired in Resolute. The airport and the hard sloping hills surrounding it were covered with driven snow. The grey skies that crowded in on the small settlement did not look promising. We were two days behind schedule.

Despite what I had been told, our equipment had arrived. Thanks to the tireless crew at Polar Shelf, all of it had been slung beneath the Coast Guard helicopter and ferried out in a series of netted loads to the ship. It was waiting on board when we arrived, a small mountain of boxes, cases and crates.

The captain of the *Pierre Radisson*, Paul Pelland, and his crew were all French-Canadian. He welcomed us in his cabin, laughing at the recollection of our surprise visit two years earlier.

"The ship is yours," Pelland said. "We will do everything we can to help you with your work. Our first job is to escort a small tanker from Resolute through the ice to the open water not far from Beechey Island. Once we get through the polar pack, we will take you up to Beechey."

Captain Pelland and his ship had had a busy summer. Since July, they had been on a series of assignments that included a trip to Tanquarry Fjord — only nine hundred and fifty-seven kilometers from the North Pole — to off-load five hundred and eighteen barrels of fuel and eleven tonnes of cargo to supply a British expedition that was headed for the North Pole. The captain, who had celebrated his forty-ninth birthday on this voyage, had been working for the Coast Guard since 1953. This was his twenty-fifth trip into the Arctic.

The sea had been Paul Pelland's life. He had grown up in a small village twenty-seven kilometers downriver from Quebec City, the ship's home port. He had taken his first command some nine years ago, a small cargo-tanker. He was fluently bilingual; he spoke to his crew in a resonant French-Canadian and talked to his new visitors in perfect English. Behind his handsome face with its trim beard was the voice of authority.

Most of the first day on board was spent unpacking our equipment and positioning it around the ship. Chris decided he would launch and recover the remotely piloted vehicle from the starboard bow area using a nine-tonne deck-crane. One deck down he set up his main control station, which included the control unit with its colour TV monitor, the power unit, and the remote controls for the vehicle propulsion system. In a small workshop nearby, Emory and Al cleared off some benches and laid out their video recorders. While everyone was busy getting to know the crew and setting up equipment, the *Pierre Radisson* pushed

151

eastward, bullying her way through the polar ice. Not far behind, following in our white broken wake, was the *Simaco*, a small oil tanker.

The next day, strong winds gusted across the ship and the sea bristled with ice. The barometer fell. In spite of the advancing storm, by late morning we were in position south of Beechey Island.

As soon as we had Beechey's black cliffs in sight, Peter Zimolong climbed into the ship's helicopter and flew off to set up his remote shore stations. On his return he went up to the ship's bridge and positioned his computer on a small table. By noon the first signals were flashing across its screen. A few seconds later the ship's track was being plotted out on the recorder. Within minutes we were directly over the *Breadalbane*.

The weather worsened. "It's gusting up to thirty knots," said the first mate, glancing at the wind indicator. The sea around the ship was covered with meter-thick slabs of ice. Pushed by the wind, they slammed into the side of the ice-breaker as it tried to hold its position over the *Breadalbane*.

The ship's meteorologist, Orest Werenka, a sea-ice specialist with the Department of the Environment, was assigned to the *Pierre Radisson* for this voyage. He held little optimism for tomorrow's forecast. "It's the first real storm of the season," he said. "North of here, in Jones Sound, the *John A. Macdonald* is having a real time of it. Close to their anchorage, waves are breaking fifty meters up on the shore. On board ship, the storm has damaged some equipment and injured one man."

We had a quick conference. "The wind is gusting up over forty knots now," said Emory. "There's a good chance we're going to get blown right out of here."

"The skipper's doing an unbelievable job just holding us in position," murmured Al Chandler.

Phil Nuytten chimed in. "How about jury-rigging a "quick-look" camera — just in case?"

We all agreed. If we couldn't use the remotely piloted vehicle, we might at least be able to drop a small camera over the side and try for whatever pictures we could get.

Shrugging into our parkas, we went down to the foredeck and began to work. A cable had to be uncoiled and connected into a small low-light level camera. "Even this package will give us much better images than we got last year," said Emory. He clapped his hands together to keep warm.

That afternoon on the deck the cold was a living thing, carried on the wind. Raw and ruthless, it mauled the faces and hands of the men who stamped their feet or thrashed their arms against their sides.

A few minutes later, in the lee of the deck-crane, Emory had a heated discussion with Al. "We have to risk it. If we lose the camera, we lose it." Al shook his head and walked away.

Emory strode over to the side of the ship and looked down at the watery wasteland. Huge pieces of ice, sharp-edged and bristling, drifted past. Weighing thousands of kilograms, any one of them could have crushed the cable. "If we lose it," said Emory to no one in particular, "someday it'll be a diver's prize." A gust of wind ripped the last words from his lips.

Within an hour, the camera and its cable were lowered over the side. The wind swerved to the northeast and blew steadily at forty knots. Occasionally there was a gust to fifty. The ship faced into the wind. The ice pans pressed hard against the hull, banging and clattering back towards the stern. Thin black lines of water showed between the pans. The cable strummed hard against the ice.

Emory lifted a fist and let it fall by his side. "Goddamn ice," he shouted. "It's never right. When we want to get down to the ship, there's too much of it. When we want to build a camp, there's not enough of it."

Al's neck bulged as he shifted his eyes to watch the cable. "We're going to lose it Emory. Let's pull her up."

I looked at Emory. He glanced out at a hideous grey mass of cloud in the distance. The brunt of his gaze was on the ice, as if his will would cause it to separate and release the cable.

I remembered the time he explained to me why he took risks.

"It's the only way to do things no one else has done. For me, pictures are everything; art, magic and information. Above all, information. And to get the good ones, you have to take risks."

The air around the ship seemed to reverberate in the growing darkness. A long ominous swell rolled under the ice.

"It's time lads. Let's bring her back up." Cursing filled the air as all hands bent to the task of pulling up the cable and coiling it into a large figure eight on the deck. The camera came in last. Before the last drops of water had fallen to the freezing deck, the men had gone, scattering to the warmth of coffee and heated cabins. Except for the crashing of ice against the hull, the deck was silent.

CHAPTER SEVENTEEN

T he next morning the sun flamed across a mirrored sea. The winds, having chased all the ice to the west except for a few scattered pans, had vanished.

The ship floated patiently on top of its own reflection about two kilometers south of the island. "I don't know who among you has the right connections," beamed the captain, "but right after breakfast we'll take advantage of this fine weather and position our anchors so that you can go down and take a look at your ship."

The emergency camera was carried to one side of the deck and everyone's attention focused on Chris's small vehicle. It sat in its launch frame, round and yellow, ready for work. Slung beneath it were four small propellers. A fifth propeller that made it ascend or descend, was housed in a central cylinder. Along its forward side were four small searchlights. Between them, like two unblinking eyes, were the still and television cameras.

Vehicles such as this one were changing the face of diving. They descended to cold, dark places forbidden to humans and stayed for long periods. They could survey, photograph, light, sample and measure. Some vehicles like this one seemed almost human.

Chris and his team took most of the day to prepare the vehicle for the dive. They inspected and tested each component. This was the first time their precious invention had been lowered this deep into the ocean depths.

Captain Pelland used the time to position the ice-breaker. Pacing back and forth across the bridge he ordered two four-tonne anchors to be lowered down, one in front of the *Breadalbane* and one behind it. Once they were in position he tightened up his anchor chains so that his ship was snug between them. Then he turned on his bow-thrusters. Using his fathomer as an underwater radar system, he urged the *Pierre Radisson* slowly forward until its bow was just aft of the stern of the *Breadalbane*.

When the vehicle was finally ready, the deck-crane lifted it up into the clear Arctic air, over the side and down into a still and somber sea.

155

Occasionally we could hear the lazy thunder of a stray ice pan banging onto the steel hull.

"Nothing to worry about," said Captain Pelland. "I'll have the boys keep the ice away." A small metal boat was lowered from its davits and began to bump the offenders away from the cable.

We lowered the vehicle into the water with great care. Its downward journey of one hundred meters would be equal in distance to a thirty-three storey building. After the vehicle splashed through the surface and started down, we rushed below deck to watch the descent on television.

During the day, Al Chandler and Gary Hayward had wired the vehicle's television camera into the ship's closed circuit system. Throughout the *Pierre Radisson*, in the crew's mess and other locations, were five television sets. The men gathered around, not wanting to miss what was happening in the darkness, deep below their ship.

As the vehicle descended, its lights were switched on. The television screen filled with swirling dots, curtains of plankton drifting on the current.

"For a cold ocean it's sure alive," someone murmured. I remembered what Rick Hoos, the Arctic marine biologist, had once told me. "The plankton growth in Lancaster Sound is about ten times more than in any other Arctic region of Canada. In turn, the plankton supports large numbers of fish, sea birds and mammals. It's no wonder that some people call Lancaster Sound an arctic oasis."

A dimly lit horizon of cobbles and small pebbles appeared on the screen. The vehicle was almost on the bottom. Chris barked out instructions to slow the descent and the vehicle touched down gently.

We waited impatiently as Chris ran through a series of system checks. Through a partially open hatchway came the tang of fresh sea air and diesel exhaust. One of the switches that Chris pressed released a jet of compressed air. The restraining bar which held the vehicle securely in its launch frame lifted up. The propellers beneath the vehicle began to spin. Slowly Chris brought the vehicle out of its frame until it was free in the water. It drove forward for about two meters and then stopped, hovering.

As if guided by some internal force, the vehicle turned on its own axis and looked back on its launch frame.

Snaking through the water were the neat coils of the vehicle's buoyant tether. The vehicle turned again, facing away from its launch frame and into the dark void of the sea. It began to cruise forward, a few meters above the bottom.

"What the hell's that?" A piece of round timber, as big as the butt of a tree, appeared on the screen.

"A section of bowsprit?"

"Maybe it's one of the yards."

The vehicle stopped and hovered over the large section of wood, examining its length and grain. It was smooth and beautifully rounded. A few meters away, at the edge of the pool of light, two pieces of straight timber jutted up from the sea floor. The vehicle swam over and shone its lights down on a pair of crosstrees.

"We're looking at the third mast," I said. "That's where a lower section of mast is connected to the one above it."

The vehicle paused, flashed its strobe-light several times and inched forward. The water was shadowy. Sensing something high and dark overhead, the vehicle hesitated. It had found the curving hull of the *Breadalbane*.

Pausing, the vehicle began a slow horizontal track a few meters above the sea floor. Its lights played across thin green plates — copper sheathing that protected the hull. At the end of its track it found the sternpost, the aftermost timber of the ship. Fixed to the post were two thick metal rings, the gudgeons that held the rudder in place. The rudder was gone.

In the old days, when a wind-ship was beset in the ice, the captain ordered the men to unship the rudder. This took the strain off the hinges and protected it from the ice.

A few seconds later the vehicle found the rudder. It was lying on its side, its hinge-pins or pintles, stabbing into the dark water. It was sheathed in copper, its surface perfectly intact.

A century ago, copper plates were nailed to the bottom of wooden ships to protect them against *Toredo Navalis*, a large wood-boring worm. Sheathing a ship improved its sailing qualities; a layer of copper was far more resistant to barnacles and weeds than bare wood. An additional preservative, a grisly mixture of tar and horsehair, was spread between the sheathing and the wood.

Cautiously, Chris steered his vehicle up the side of the *Breadalbane*. He was afraid of becoming entangled, fouling the vehicle or its cable in the wreckage. Occasionally he spun the vehicle slowly on its own axis so that it looked back to make sure that its tether was clear of any obstruction.

Lying against the port side of the *Breadalbane* was a collection of broken spars and smashed railing. Steering past this tangle, stopping to record it on film, Chris worked his way up towards the bow. He stayed under the curve of the hull next to the copper sheathing. Patches of orange and pink coral appeared on the screen. Colonies had attached themselves to the places where the copper had fallen away.

The coral was part of a mélange of marine invertebrates that had invaded the ship. The camera, moving up the side of the hull, revealed

157

clusters of sea-stars, anemones and purple sea urchins. Up near the bulwarks and railing, more exposed to the current, were additional colonies. Scattered among them were mussels and clams, brittle stars and, where the railing met the deck, the ghost-white arms of a basket star.

The dominant colour was the orange and pink of thick branches of soft coral. As the vehicle backed up for a wider view, it seemed that the ship was aflame. Bill Mason, who was filming over Chris's shoulder, let out a low, admiring whistle.

The sky was growing dark. Reluctantly we lifted the vehicle from the water.

That night we celebrated our first visit to the *Breadalbane*. In the Officer's lounge our glasses were charged and the toasts began.

The star of the evening was Paul Pelland. The captain had held his ship over the *Breadalbane* for more than three hours. In his quiet, authoritative manner he had dominated the bridge, forcing the *Radisson* to behave like a precision instrument.

The next morning was spent charging batteries, adding hydraulic oil, loading film and running down a ten-page checklist. By noon we were ready.

But the tide was not.

"We had better wait for it to go slack," Pelland said. "It should take about two hours."

In spite of our eagerness to dive we knew we had to wait. When the tide was running, it made the ship hard to hold in position. Too strong a current and the *Radisson* would drag one of its four-tonne anchors right into the *Breadalbane*.

The weather held. A scattering of high clouds lay far to the south. Light breezes floated down from Devon Island and rippled the water. The ice, a long line of unruly pans, lurked in the distance.

In spite of meticulous preparations, the first dive was aborted. The slim metal bar that held the vehicle in its frame would not release. Everything was hauled back up to the surface.

The problem was quickly found. A small air cylinder was replaced. Within the hour we were back on the bottom.

This time the bar released and the vehicle flew out of its cage and headed toward the sunken ship. The water ahead, bathed in light, was filled with silver dots of plankton. The vehicle picked its way slowly over the fallen debris: shattered timber, broken yards, fragments of hand-hewn elm and pine. Working its way towards the bow, it discovered the anchor.

The large iron fluke, partially buried in the sea floor, was barely discernible. It was covered with a thin layer of crusted growth.

In the shadows behind the anchor, looming in the darkness, was the bow of the *Breadalbane*. The vehicle turned slowly and shone its light upward. Somewhere, just out of range, tucked under the bowsprit, was the figure-head.

"Damn. I can't get any closer." Chris's face was pinched. "I've run out of tether. I'll have to bring her back."

The vehicle spun slowly and followed its tether back towards the stern. As he worked, Chris was forming a mental image of the *Breadalbane*, trying to remember each piece of debris and its relationship to the ship. A small miscalculation and he would entangle his vehicle.

Once he was clear of the wreckage, he let the vehicle drift until it was sitting quietly at rest on the ocean floor.

"Unbelievable machine, isn't she?" beamed Chris.

He was right. The vehicle had been underwater for more than two hours. If a diver had been down at the same depth, taking pictures for the same length of time, he would be cold, exhausted and accident prone. In addition, he would be faced with about ten hours of decompression.

"Okay, let's take a look at one of the masts."

He lifted the vehicle about five meters off the floor of the ocean and moved it slowly back towards the hull. The lights passed over the railing, throwing them into shadow. After a few minutes of searching, Chris found the wooden base of the mainmast. The vehicle began to climb. The lower portion of the mast was clear of marine life. But higher up, at the junction of crosstrees and trusses, the sea-growth was luxuriant. Everyone's eyes strained forward trying to discern a hint of furled canvas.

Caught in the current, the vehicle drifted away.

Suddenly it jerked to a stop. "Damn," whispered Chris. He shifted nervously in his seat and leaned in closer to the television screen.

The vehicle turned on its axis and peered back along the length of its tether. Like a floating slinky-toy the tether trailed off into the shadowy water near the mast. Somehow it had become fouled.

The room was silent. Chris's hands were wrapped around the control box, his knuckles white. Keeping the base of the mast in view, he re-traced the vehicle's path through the water. Chris flew it cautiously, instinctively, keeping a slight tension in the line. With infinite patience he pulled the machine free.

"That was close."

"Cool lad Chris."

"Nice going. We've got it all on tape."

Later in the dive Chris ran the vehicle down the starboard side of the hull and discovered the huge hole that had been smashed in by the ice over a hundred years ago. It was easy to see why the ship had gone down so quickly. Through the jagged opening, we could see a forest of broken timbers. Beneath them lay what remained of the cargo.

The vehicle backed up and headed towards the stern. Riding on its wash it rose past the transom, the taffrail, the main deck and the square outline of the deck-house. It paused for a moment. And then we saw it. In front of the lights, bathed in yellow, was the ship's wheel.

I held my breath. Here it was, massive and circular, the very heart of the ship. After years of searching, we had found it, its old spoked handles once grasped by human hands, now ablaze with garlands of coral. And what hands they must have been, strong-fingered, and salt-cut, worked by big shoulders and hearts that would never stop.

In front of the wheel, a few steps across the deck, were the flat roof and walls of the deck-house. On either side, two doors with open windows, led into the dark interior. Between them, hanging on the wall, was a large open-shelf cabinet. The vehicle drifted in closer, its lights playing across the old timbers and their living tapestry of colour. On the cabinet's lower shelf, securely cradled, was a small signal lantern. Its glass was intact, its metal frame green with age. What young arms had held that lantern aloft in the dark wildness of an Atlantic storm? Who had placed it back in its cradle for the final time?

Beside the lantern was the ship's compass. A few hundred kilometers from the north magnetic pole, its needle was perfectly still.

My heart raced. Who was the last human being to look at that compass. The master? The mate? One of the sailors?

As the vehicle drew back, I saw on the deck and in the deck-house the ghosts of a dim, long ago time — the men of the *Breadalbane*. Some were slogging through their daily chores. Some were wolfing food from small bowls. Others were wrapped in woolen blankets, snoring in their bunks.

Here were the spirits of sailors, young and old, who had battled the wild Atlantic and fought their way into the Arctic. A century separated us. A century that included two World Wars, an explosion of technology, and the shadow of nuclear destruction.

And yet the men on board the *Radisson* and all the others involved in this search were not so different from the crew of the *Breadalbane*. They shared a sense of hope, independence and trust. They were joined by a spirit of adventure. These human characteristics transcended social and political changes, carrying us back through the centuries and forward into the future.

The vehicle remained at the window for a long time, looking in, as if trying to gain entrance. The lights played with shadows. Then it slowly withdrew and moved across the deck. The light receded. It was time to return.

Once again, the *Breadalbane*, its wheel motionless, its compass stilled, its bowsprit pointing eastward towards England and home, was shrouded in darkness.

CHAPTER EIGHTEEN

J une, 1982. For the seventh time in as many years I flew back to Beechey Island, this time to film a television special. Even this late in the year, at the beginning of the arctic summer, ice dominated everything. From the air it appeared to be lifeless and inert. But I knew differently.

Over the years, I had seen this most formidable of barriers at close hand, above and below its troubled surface. It was nothing less than a miracle that, in spite of its unyielding nature, it had opened up briefly — long enough for me to find the *Breadalbane*.

The discovery was an achievement of many people, some who had actually taken part in the search and some who had never even seen the Arctic.

Since 1970 this frozen ocean and its mantle of ice had become a special challenge, an Everest that I felt compelled to climb. The real Everest had once been described in a way that seemed to suit the arctic ice: "It is never conquered. Occasionally it allows a momentary success."

I breathed a long sigh of satisfaction. After three years of trying, I had found a ship buried for over a century under an ocean of ice. I had survived the rigours of fund-raising, the frustrations of failure, and the long lines of people who said it couldn't be done.

Effortlessly, the aircraft turned and banked towards the west. I thought, "One day I will dive down to my ship. Now that I've found her, I want to reach out and touch her."

Up ahead loomed a long line of grey clouds and beyond them the crimson flash of the midnight sun. Behind me, fading like a speck in the distance, was the island, the ice, and an unfinished dream.

For a long time I secretly believed that my dream of putting a man on the deck of the *Breadalbane* — a working diver using the world's most advanced underwater technology — would remain forever unfulfilled. In 1981 and again in 1982 we planned large and complex diving operations from a camp built on the ice over the ship. Each year a reconnaissance by aircraft revealed a shattered ocean — a chaos of broken and tumbled ice blocks. Each year the expedition had to be postponed. Months of planning, weeks of preparations, with equipment leased and supplies ready for shipping, came to an abrupt stop. It was beginning to look as if the frozen ocean had a permanent lock on the ship.

Worse yet, the technical and financial support needed for such a costly and complicated expedition was beginning to evaporate. After two years of waiting for "the big one," even the most ardent supporters were beginning to lose interest and move on to other projects.

To maintain interest, I wrote a book called *The Breadalbane Adventure* which was first published in December, 1982, and I hoped that its publication would help to sustain interest in the project.

Like all captives of a dream, I was determined not to give up. However, after talking to ice experts in Ottawa and Calgary, I decided to change my strategy. Since the pressure ridges that formed over the ship each year were the biggest problem, we would have to learn more about them. What were their shape and thickness? How fast did they move? To find the answers to these and other questions, I began to organize an expedition that would focus, not on the *Breadalbane*, but on the unpredictable white barrier that lay between us and the sunken ship.

Early in 1983, preparations for a scaled-down expedition were under way. Our objectives were simple. A four-man camp would be set up on the shore-fast ice next to Beechey Island. A weather station to measure temperature, wind strength, and direction would be established. Time-lapse photographs of the ice would be made. Precision theodoletes would be used to detect movement of the pressure ridges. A sector-scanning sonar would be used to map the underwater configuration of the ice. We hoped to obtain enough weather and sea-ice data to allow the diving-science program to be carried out in 1984.

But once again, as it had in 1981, a phone call from Resolute Bay changed everything. It came from the camp set up by the Canada Centre for Inland Waters, a scientific group doing ice and current studies in Barrow Strait to the west of Beechey Island. It was from my old friend, engineer Ed Lewis. This time his voice had more colour in it. "This year's ice around Beechey looks pretty good," he said. "There are pressure ridges, but they seem smaller. And you'll be happy to hear there are some flat areas between them."

A few days later I studied aerial photographs sent down by mail from Resolute. Ed was right. There were lots of pressure ridges, but there were also plenty of smooth areas in between. I couldn't tell from the pictures exactly where the *Breadalbane* lay, but I had a hunch. This was the year. It had to be. Looking at the shadowy ridges stitched across the ice and the small, flat patches of white between them, I prayed that one of those patches lay over the ship. I was about to take the biggest gamble of my life.

CHAPTER NINETEEN

April, 1983. "What do you think?" His eyes were tight to the window, fastened on the sea ice speeding under the wingtip at more than two hundred kilometers an hour, three hundred feet below. A smile slipped onto Pete Jess's clean-shaven face. "Anyway, in a few hours we'll know for sure."

The Twin Otter banked and turned away from Beechey's snow-dusted cliffs. In spite of the brilliant sunshine outside the window the temperature was minus 20 degrees Celsius. A few minutes later we were standing on the ice in our parkas, next to the aircraft, inspecting the damaged tail skid. Harry Hanlon, the big, red-bearded pilot, leaned forward. "A little bumpy," he said to no one in particular. Running a gloved hand over the twisted metal, he glanced up and inspected the aluminum tail. "I've seen a lot worse."

Harry was one of those men whose twin-engined aircraft shrank the Arctic down to a manageable size. His skills and laconic approach to life would have elevated him to the captain's cabin of a nineteenth-century sailing ship. Listening to our worried talk about the ice, he shifted his weight from one foot to the other and looked out across the rumpled white surface of the ocean. "You guys have it all wrong," he said in that Right Stuff, voice-of-the-pilot tone. Sea ice is unpredictable because it has a soul." Pete Jess, a man with eleven years of arctic experience as a helicopter pilot and logistics expert, looked up at the sky.

"O.K., Harry, tell us how you know."

"It's simple. Now you take icebergs, for example. The past few years they've been staying in the fjords, holding back." A gust of wind tugged at Pete's hat. "Icebergs are not as aggressive as they used to be — they've lost their initiative. That's the reason we've had no more *Titanics*. I've got a theory that the really big icebergs are lying low, waiting until we get more oil rigs working in deeper water."

"You know what I think, Harry? You been inhaling too many exhaust fumes."

Harry had put us down on the ice about two kilometers southeast of Beechey Island. Somewhere to the west, under flat ice or the spine of a pressure ridge, lay the *Breadalbane*. Our first job was to pinpoint its position. For two hours we remained next to the aircraft, keeping an eye out for polar bears, while the real work was being done in the distance. As we watched, a small red and white helicopter, a Bell Jet Ranger, landed at Cape Riley and a young man with a moustache and anxious eyes jumped out. He ran out from under the whirling blades and trudged across the snow to plant a precision instrument on a tripod firmly in the snow. It was Brian McKillop, age twenty-eight, a technician from Telefix Canada, who was responsible for refinding the *Breadalbane*. As the key member of the advance team, he knew that nothing could happen — neither camp construction, cutting of the ice holes, nor underwater operations — until the ship was clearly in view. McKillop's job was to place us directly above it so that we could cut a hole through the ice and make visual contact with our sector-scanning sonar.

Choosing his location, McKillop set up the instrument, a push-button, microwave distance meter, on its sturdy metal stand. The MICROFIX 100C, with its self-contained battery, weighed less than four kilograms. Capable of measuring out to sixty thousand meters within five seconds, it would, if handled properly in the violent cold, be accurate within centimeters. As McKillop hefted the instrument into position on Cape Riley, he treated it with something close to affection. Leaving the first MICROFIX station he climbed back into the helicopter, and was flown over to the head of Erebus and Terror Bay, where he set up a second MICROFIX and a surveyor's theodolite. Then he was landed next to Franklin's cairn at the top of Beechey Island. The ship's location would be found by walking a third MICROFIX across the ice until it made a precise, long-distance triangle. Finding the final position took two hours of bone-chilling work.

"Are you sure?"

It was a question I hated to ask. Tiny beads of sweat, formed as he humped his equipment through the hard-packed snow, glistened on McKillop's forehead. He looked down, his boot tracing a slow circle in the snow.

"I checked it with a third measurement from Franklin's cairn."

The words came out flat and featureless. Like all good technicians, McKillop wondered what the cold and the rough usage had done to his equipment and his calculations. There was no way he could be really certain until we cut through two meters of ice and lowered the sonar.

"We'd be hard pressed to find a better spot."

"Well done, Brian. Great job."

McKillop's hard work, summarized by a small circle in the snow, had put us in a good position on the ice. To the north, towards the island, was a long ice pan as flat as a griddle, yet large enough to land a Twin Otter. Off to the east was a series of big pressure ridges. In every other direction

166

lay low, broken ice hummocks. If McKillop was right, and the ice didn't shift, the *Breadalbane* was almost a ship length away from the nearest pressure ridge.

"Absolutely nothing. No image. Nothing." Emory Kristof shook his head and knuckled his bloodshot eyes with hands raw and crimson. He stared at the small video screen sitting on a crate. A pool of melt water encircled his feet. Except for a thin line sweeping repeated electronic circles, the video screen was blank.

"The damn thing has disappeared."

A voice came from the other side of the makeshift tent: "Maybe someone — the Russians — have stolen it."

"O.K., pull up the sonar head. Let's try another hole."

Hugging themselves against the cold, a trio of bodies disappeared through a loosely fastened door.

Kristof's voice rose against the roar of the generator: "Careful of that sonar head when you haul it up on the ice."

Three days had passed since we first landed. Everything except the weather was going wrong. Aircraft-scheduling problems in Resolute had left us with fewer flights than planned. Camp construction was far behind schedule. And after cutting five holes in the area where McKillop had positioned us, and dropping the sector-scanning sonar down each one, we still had not seen the *Breadalbane*.

"It's like wrestling a fog," said Pete Jess, rubbing his hands together over the Herman Nelson heater. "If I can't get aircraft, I can't build your camp."

Pete's eyes had lost their sparkle. On the flat, one-acre site we had picked to set up the camp with its kitchen, sleeping quarters, and work tents, Pete and his three assistants Gary Luton, Ted Janulis, and my son Jeff had been everywhere at once, rolling fuel drums, putting up tent frames, starting stoves, moving snow, cutting holes. In spite of their nonstop work, we were falling behind. Looking at Pete's tightly drawn face, I thought of other men, far away, who were also putting in eighteen-hour days: Phil Nuytten and his divers in Vancouver, getting ready to ship two atmospheric diving systems; Chris Nicholson and Martin Bowen in Massachusetts, doing last-minute checks of their remotely piloted vehicle (RPV); Bill Mason and Alan Geldhart in Ottawa, loading cameras to shoot a film for the National Film Board.

"Look out, here comes the sonar head." A yellow line and electric cable leading into a small ice hole came to a stop. A pair of gloved hands pulled on the line and lifted a round black object out of the water.

Once again the success or failure of the expedition rested on a complex piece of integrated circuitry. The UDI sonar head measured thirty-four by twenty centimeters and weighed four kilograms. English-built, it

Diver Phil Nuytten returning to the surface after the first manned dive to the Breadalbane. *To the left is diver Doug Osborne, who made the next three dives and recovered the ship's wheel.*
Emory Kristof — ©National Geographic Society

Doug Osborne studying the binnacle with its contents of compasses and compass light. The binnacle is on the stern wall of the deckhouse. He decided not to take the compasses to the surface because of possible damage.
Emory Kristof — ©National Geographic Society

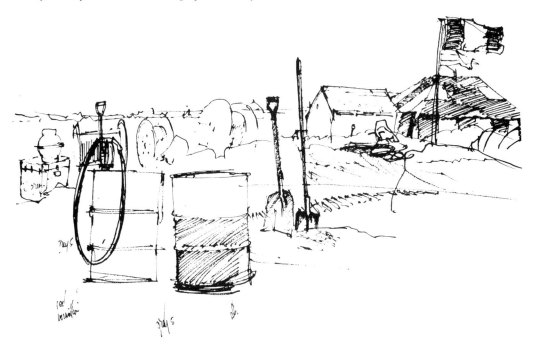

The author examines the ship's wheel shortly after its recovery to the surface. It was given to Parks Canada for conservation.
Emory Kristof — ©National Geographic Society

Campsite two kilometers off Beechey Island during the 1983 expedition. The Breadalbane *lies just above and to the right of the striped tent, one hundred meters below the ice.*
Emory Kristof — ©National Geographic Society

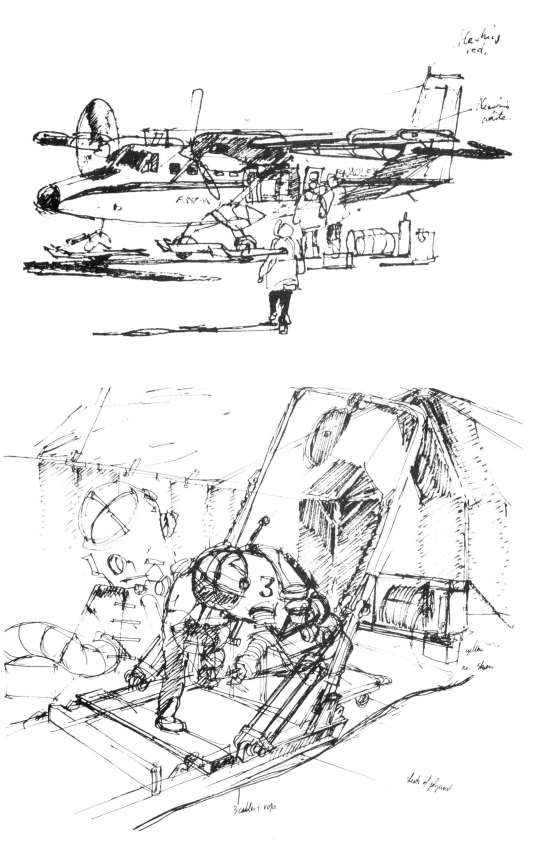

flashing
red.

flashing
white.

F.RSPAV

BRADLEY

3

yellow
nr. Shewn

3 cradles + rope

Seats of plywood

max parkell.

produced a 27-degree vertical by 1.4-degree horizontal beam width transmitted at 500 KHZ. Down near the bottom, the sonar head scanned a 360-degree circle, giving high-resolution, television-like pictures out to a distance of one hundred meters.

Kristof stomped out of the tent and pushed his big fur hat back on his head. With his boot he nudged the black head lying on the ice. A slim crack, caused by the below-zero temperatures, ran up the length of its black casing.

"Now listen, honey, I know you are doing the best job you can, but it just isn't good enough."

Kristof reached down and patted the head. The UDI sector-scanning sonar was one of his favourite image-makers. The previous spring he had used it successfully in Lake Ontario to guide his camera systems around the site of two American warships, *Hamilton* and *Scourge*, sunk in 1813. Like the *Breadalbane*, the two ships were found upright, listing slightly and almost intact except for blocks and spars that had fallen as the sails and rigging gave way.

A tall figure wearing a bright red parka and brown watchcap appeared next to Kristof. "Cactus" Ralph White, photographer, sky diver, crack shot, and ex-Marine, was a deputy sheriff in the Los Angeles Police Department. He was also one of those individuals whose hard work and wide range of talents make an expedition successful. He glared down at the sonar head.

"One more chance, baby, then ol' Ralph is gonna go for the three-oh-three and blow you away."

The two men were joined by Pete Jess. The three of them stood looking down at the water in the ice hole as if it could tell them something.

"Let's put it back in the first hole we made, the one we cut next to McKillop's position."

Without a word White picked up the sonar head, carried it across the ice, one hundred meters of cable trailing behind him, and carefully placed it in the subzero water.

"Lower away, lads. Let's see if Murphy's luck is with us."

Down below the ice the sonar dropped slowly to ten, twenty, and then fifty meters. This time, unlike previous lowerings, there was no strong current racing under the ice, pulling on the cable, deflecting the sonar head so that it faced away from the sea floor. It was slack tide and the head went straight down until it hovered twenty meters from the bottom and stopped in the quivering water.

On the video screen inside the tent the electronic line continued its monotonous circular sweep until it reached the lower left-hand corner, where it seemed to stagger and break up into fragments. The fragments went hard and white, then into a long curved line, a profile, a pattern that showed the deck, deckhouse, bow, and the stern of the *Breadalbane*.

A few days later I was sitting by the stove in the kitchen writing an entry in my journal. It was just after breakfast and the aroma of bacon and eggs still filled the air. Our chef, David Rea, busied himself with some cartons in a corner. Jeff, Ted, and Gary were hard at the dishes. At a nearby table four burly men sat talking over mugs of steaming coffee.

At the bottom of the page I wrote: ". . . spoke to the troops yesterday about the dangers of camping on sea ice and the five fears . . ."

The first fear was wind. So far we had seen little of it. In the Arctic this is wondrous blessing, for it is wind that freezes fingers, sandpapers faces with snow, and sends strong men scurrying for shelter. The calm, cold days, with the sun in the sky most of the night, allowed us to work long hours. Thanks to Peter Jess and his team, the camp was nearly complete. In addition to the kitchen, there were two other well-insulated parcolls and three double-walled tents. Inside were humming stoves and beds and workspace for more than twenty men. Outside were piles of gear, generators, drums of fuel, and Skidoos to move supplies in from the airstrip.

The second fear was a violent shift in the ice. Four years earlier, a crack as wide as a roadway had appeared in the ice beneath our camp at the North Pole. Under the force of a strong wind, sea ice could heave into pressure ridges in minutes. So far we had heard only one ominous sound: a tremendous thunderclap late at night from somewhere out in the strait.

Polar bears presented the third threat. Everyone, especially when away from the centre of camp, was continuously glancing over a shoulder. Our eyes were always in motion, studying the snow for a paw print, surveying the faraway ice for the twitch of a black-tipped snout. So far we had been lucky.

The fourth fear was ice-cold water. It was always just below us, its lethal grip hidden under two meters of ice. The big ice hole, through which we would place the atmospheric diving suit, was the size of a small pool. If someone fell in, he might be unable to recover from the heart-stopping cold.

Fire was the final fear. Flames from an overheated generator, or a spark near a fuel drum, and we could lose irreplaceable equipment and perhaps even a life. There was a fire extinguisher in every tent, but there was no water pressure and no way of calling for help. A big wind in combination with a fire could cause us to lose most of the camp.

"Let's go out and see how they're doing on the big dive hole." David Rea grinned as he slipped into his bulky parka. For a talented cook he was disarmingly slim. Tucking my note pad into my pocket, I followed him out into the brilliant sunshine.

After more than a week's work the camp was a neat row of low-roofed, red-and-white parcolls and tents. A hundred meters away, towards the airstrip, fuel drums were neatly stacked. To the south, off the starboard side of the ship a hundred meters below them, the men were cutting out the big dive hole. Working in shifts, they had hacked and shovelled endless tons of low hummocky ice until the area was level. Then Pete Jess had cut a series of holes one-third of a meter apart. Into each he had dropped a thin stick of geo-gel which, when detonated, had sent a shower of pulverized ice skyward. Pete and Ralph's expertise in getting through the ice quickly had saved us hundreds of hours of back-breaking labour. When David Rea and I arrived, the men were shovelling away the last of the fractured ice.

Two of them, Bill Mason and Claus Heinecke, a marine artist, were leaning on the handles of their shovels, catching their breath.

"What do you do, Pete, when a polar bear hangs around a camp?" Bill Mason had a good reason to ask; he was frequently away from the camp, making wide-angle shots of Beechey Island and Erebus and Terror Bay.

"You try not to shoot them," said Jess.

"But what do you do if they won't go away?"

"You can always try bear balls."

"Bear balls?" Masons's words came out in twin white puffs. Somewhere, a shovel fell with a clang on the ice.

"Yep, You roll up apple-size balls of bread and peanut butter, let them freeze, and hang them up on a two-by-four outside the camp."

"Sounds pretty appetizing to me."

"And to the bear. He gulps it down without knowing there's red-hot Tabasco Sauce hidden inside. By the time it explodes in his stomach, he's a mile away and at full gallop."

The men were in good spirits thanks to David Rea's expertise in front of the stove, we were exceedingly well-fed. The remotely piloted vehicle, star of the 1981 expedition, had arrived in good condition with its inventor Chris Nicholson and technician Martin Bowen. In a few hours His Excellency Ed Schreyer, Governor General of Canada, on a tour of the Arctic, would arrive to inspect the camp. He would find twenty-three tired but highly motivated men. If the weather held, the first manned dives to the ship were only a few days away. As an expression of their boundless energy the youngest members of the team, Ted, Jeff, and Gary, had taken some spare lumber and a small stove and constructed something that every well-founded Arctic expedition should have — a sauna.

The fire started sometime after midnight, a bright orange flame licking up from behind the brown metal stove in the third parcoll. A few feet away, surrounded by duffle bags and boots, eight men, exhausted after a long day, slept a deep and peaceful sleep. Over their heads, clotheslines strung from the frame of the parcoll were festooned with shirts, socks, and trousers hung up to dry. The flame grew, leaping higher, feeding on the pool of kerosene in the drip pan, up past the hair-line crack in the thin copper tubing. Less than a body length away, on the other side of the thin fabric wall, was a forty-five-gallon fuel drum.

The man sleeping in the cot next to the stove awoke with a start, his nostrils filled with the acrid stench of smoke. He shook his head as if in a dream and then saw it, the orange-yellow flame between the stove and the wall. Mike Cole, an electronic technician from *The National Geographic*, a slender man in his mid-thirties, sat up and flung back the cover of his sleeping bag. Landing his feet on the ice-cold floor, he groped in the darkness for the small fire extinguisher lying next to some boxes. He didn't see it, just felt its hard metal case under his fingers. From some recess in his brain he remembered: hold it upright, pull the pin, and squeeze the trigger. A bitter cloud of white dust sprayed out of the nozzle. The flames fell and seemed to disappear. Other men were sitting up now, some of them rubbing their eyes. There was alarm in their voices. Bent on fetching another fire extinguisher, a man, completely naked except for some boots, sprang out the door into the minus-30-degree night.

Cole began to cough, but he leaned forward to peer at the base of the stove. A sudden hellfire burst of flame drove him back, but he pointed the cannister again and fired another salvo and then another as the flames lifted and tried to outflank the stream of powder. A figure appeared outside the window, his hands wrestling with the fuel-line shut-off valve. Barely able to breathe, Cole fired still another burst at the base of the stove and saw the flame die. Holding his breath, he staggered towards the door and fresh air.

Two men with fresh fire extinguishers went inside, but the fire was finished. A man's arm went around Mike Cole's shoulder, another around his waist. They guided him towards the kitchen. After some coffee and quiet conversation, the men dispersed to sleep on the floor of the other parcolls. It was one-fifteen in the morning of April 27. Mike Cole, coughing intermittently from the pain in his chest, went back to his deep and peaceful sleep.

As in 1981, the RPV, with its quartz iodide lights and twin cameras, was our roving eye on the *Breadalbane*. It's omnidirectional mobility and underwater endurance made it a perfect companion to the divers. On the bottom it would light their way and monitor their movements. It would allow us to observe and record everything that happened. If the diver had an emergency, such as entanglement, the RPV, with its new manipulator arm, would be invaluable. My plan was to let the remotely piloted vehicle precede the divers into the depths, recording important landmarks, saving precious time. We would have four days of RPV dives before the first manned dive.

"Can you hold it there, right next to the ice?" In the dim light of the

RPV control tent biologist John Roff leaned over Martin Bowen's shoulder and stared hard at the video screen. The foreground filled with an eddy of ice crystals and white dots. In the background lay a spur of deep-draught ice.

Bowen flicked two switches on the hand control; the RPV slowed and then stopped. Roff, a marine biologist from the University of Guelph, had been coming to the Arctic for two years to study its algae, the primary energy producers in the food chain. He had taken time out from his own work to join us so that he could get his first look at the under-ice world with a remotely piloted camera.

"What are we looking at?" asked Bowen, squinting at the swirling dots.

"Algae." Roff paused and then continued as if talking to a class on campus.

"In the polar oceans, algae grows within the lower layers of ice where it forms a thin, yellow-green carpet. Here, in the Northwest Passage, it begins to grow as soon as the sun comes up in February. By June, just before the ice breaks up, it becomes really dense. In fact, nowhere else in the oceans is there such an incredible biomass of algae."

Some of the dots danced off the screen. Bowen slowly panned the video camera upwards so that Roff could better see the ceiling of algae. Warmed by such an intimate view of his subject, Roff continued.

"Some of the algae is eaten by small grazing animals, but most of it falls, sinking to the sea floor where it feeds the benthos — the animals on the bottom."

Roff had seen some of the colour photographs of the *Breadalbane*, taken two years earlier. What had struck him was the variety of species growing on the mast, deck, and railings.

"From what I have seen, the *Breadalbane* is colonized exclusively by animals. Most of them are filter feeders collecting particles, including algae, suspended in the water around them. The dominant forms, providing the ship with much of its intense colour, are soft corals."

As the RPV began to move down from the ice, the video screen filled again with a blizzard of dots. This part of the Northwest Passage was only a few weeks away from the annual breakup. Down on the *Breadalbane*, a steady fall of algae, as it had for more than a century, was sustaining a layer of life.

John Roff and Martin Bowen spent more than an hour together, one piloting, the other watching, each man exploring a world he had never seen before. For Bowen, the challenge was to ensure that the RPV was in perfect trim before the first descent to the ship. For Roff, the challenge was the new technology: how he could use it to learn more about the biomass and energy within the polar ocean.

For the man struggling across the ice about five miles west of the RPV, there was a completely different challenge: how to stay awake. Tom

Wallace, his eyes stinging after more than twenty-four hours without sleep, stared out through the frosty front window of his D-6 Caterpillar tractor. His ears rang with the roar of the 300-horsepower engine and the clatter of steel treads marching across the ice. His muscles ached. After driving more than a hundred and fifty non-stop kilometers between Resolute Bay and Beechey Island — bouncing, banging, sliding, scraping — Wallace was fighting off an overwhelming urge to sleep.

Traced out in the snow and stretching into the hazy distance behind him was a narrow, twin-rutted track that he had made along the shore of Cornwallis Island and the sea ice of Barrow Strait and Wellington Channel. Ahead of him, clearly visible, were the stark cliffs of Beechey Island. Somewhere below those cliffs was a campsite with warmth, food, and rest.

Wallace kept awake by amusing himself with thoughts about the strangeness of his situation. Four days ago he had been sunning himself on the deck of his sailboat at the marina in Sydney, British Columbia. As his wife Linda handed him the phone, she whispered, "It's from Resolute."

"Tom, we're finally ready. We've got to get two diving suits, a big winch and compresser, about fifteen tonnes, out to the site. We've got your old D-6 cat, two wheel-equipped sleds, and an airline ticket for you. Can you help us?"

Wallace smiled. A promise made . . . and here he was, a man retired, pounding himself to pieces in the cab of an iron machine that had a top speed of four kilometers an hour.

The Cat clanked to a stop and a familiar fear fluttered into Wallace's stomach. If a crack in the ice occurred, he would fall a distance that equalled the height of a fifty-storey building. He had to keep moving in order to distribute the weight of the load. He carefully backed the machine a few paces and dropped the blade into position. Then he jammed the Cat into low gear and lurched forward. He had long ago lost track of how far he had come and how many of these low ridges he had had to scrape level. All he knew was that the camp was up ahead and perhaps in an hour . . . or maybe two . . .

Since that day, five years ago, when he first set foot on Beechey Island and saw Northumberland House and the graves of Franklin's men, Phil Nuytten had dreamed of this moment. In his mind, and in the minds of the support team that worked on the ice above him, the age of Franklin was still alive. And now, hanging in the water under the ice, Nuytten was about to dive down to the ship that, for him, best symbolized that age.

Nuytten was alone under a frozen sea in the armoured suit he had helped to design. Called WASP because of its insect-like shape and yellow colour, it would allow him to descend to the sea floor and still remain at surface pressure. Tethered by a slim black cable and powered by six thrusters, WASP could literally "fly" in the water. Nuytten was dressed in two layers of thick underwear, and after wrestling the suit through the ice hole he was warm. He wiped the sweat off his forehead and extended his wool-clad arms into hollow conduits that bent freely under pressure and allowed him to operate a pair of rotating-grip manipulators. After checking his oxygen and carbon dioxide indicators, he took a deep breath and leaned back in the clear acrylic dome to take in the view. The water was transparent, shading from a soft blue in front of him to a deep navy and then, directly below him, midnight black.

"Hey, Phil, you asleep?" Doug Osborne's voice crackled over the intercom.

"Er . . . no, Doug, just finishing a systems check at ten meters."

"O.K. All set up here to lower you down."

"Roger that. Lower away."

As he descended, Nuytten searched the water above and below. Because of the luminous glow of the ice, the upward view was more comforting. To his right, the suit's umbilical cable dwindled away to a thread. There were bright blue patches where the snow had been cleared around the big dive tent. Directly overhead, the dive hole glowed like a postage stamp.

Nuytten looked down again and out of the corner of his eye saw a massive spear tip jutting up in the blackness: one of the masts of the *Breadalbane*, growing thicker, the crosstree going by. Then suddenly, softly, he was on the forward roof of the deckhouse on the port side, next to a hand-carved railing and a fallen spar.

Now his mind was in high gear — Nuytten the diver, Nuytten the totem-pole carver, the lover of sea life and maritime history, taking in the most stunning underwater vista he had ever seen.

Even in twilight, the ship was far bigger than he imagined, far bigger than what was seen on television or in still pictures — a great black ghost of a thing, the sweep of its deck reaching out on all sides of him.

He turned and saw the lights of the RPV coming through the water. It was not far away and he followed it as it worked its way slowly through the wreckage of the drowned ship. A part of his mind tried to keep track of his umbilical cable somewhere overhead, dangerously close to the masts.

He leaned forward, his face almost touching the acrylic dome, to look down through openings in the roofboards into the deckhouse. It was a big space, like a framed house, partitioned into rooms filled with benches and tables and chairs. Over a century of tidal current had done its work and the wood looked sandblasted, the hard brown grain standing out in the lights. The ends of some of the wall planks showed tool marks. There were no telltale holes to indicate that *Toredo*, the great leveller of all wooden ships, had survived in the Arctic.

Nuytten stayed there for a long time, mostly in silence, sometimes talking quietly to Doug Osborne more than a third of a kilometer above him. Trying to gauge the direction and strength of the current, Nuytten clicked on his forward thrusters and moved cautiously towards the stern. He dropped off the roof of the deckhouse and flew just off the side of the ship. Even though he had made thousands of dives all over the world, the colour and clarity of this scene left him speechless. Afterwards he would describe the ship as a luxuriant garden raised off the sea floor, filled with saffron basket stars and splashes of scarlet and orange. Below was the copper-plated hull, a high, curved wall of turquoise. Spars, timbers, railings, and yards, ranging in colour from tan to mahogany, were strewn everywhere. The entire ship was framed by a sea of cobalt blue.

Nuytten was still warm, but he could feel the ocean's cold pressing through the metal of the suit, steaming up the inside of the acrylic. He kept wiping the dome, working the thrusters, putting his hands down into the arms of the suit, bending them gently to ensure that they would keep working in the cold. Frequently he thought of all the men on the surface: technicians, life support, specialists, listening to his voice, tending his lines, watching him on television. At intervals one of those men went outside the tent and read a pair of MICROFIX instruments to see if there had been any movement in the ice.

For two years Nuytten had been looking at an object in black-and-white and colour photographs and now, if he was careful, he would be able to see it up close: the ship's wheel. To get to it, he had to fly a specific course over wreckage that was piled up in the stern. After several tries he figured it out: he had to fly out over the transom, turn completely around, and then fly back over the transom on the starboard side. As soon as the deck was directly below, the forward thruster had to be secured, the down thruster engaged, and the umbilical cable slacked. With awkward grace, Nuytten dropped the suit into a confined space slightly to one side of the wheel.

He dared not stay too long. The vicious cold outside and the increasing moisture inside the suit was freezing the surface of his wool underwear to the metal. He was concerned what the tide, coming off slack, might be doing to his umbilical. And he was tired; he had been submerged for more than an hour.

He steadied the suit on its yellow butt and then gently leaned it forward, staring hard at the wheel and the box binnacle attached to the rear wall of the deckhouse. He could pick up details that could not otherwise be seen: the wood everywhere so thin, the metal fastenings so fragile after years of corrosion, the compasses nestled deep in their cubicles, the wheel, odd-angled, as if it had fallen free of its attachment.

Finally it was time to leave and he backed away, reluctantly telling

Osborne that he was coming up, working his way free of the debris, clear of the wreck and the masts, until the ice was overhead and the ship down in the darkness below him. Then he wriggled through the ice hole and was on the surface, back in the diesel roar of the tent, the dome swinging open, men shouting, hands reaching in and helping him out.

By the afternoon of May 5 we had made three manned dives to the *Breadalbane*. The RPV, which had made five dives, had brought back a treasure trove of more than twelve hundred still-frame photographs. On each dive it had descended through a separate ice hole, dropped one hundred meters to the sea floor, and made its way carefully over fallen yards and timbers to the ship's hull. Repeated hard use in cold water had taken a toll: the machine had kept burning out its vertical thruster. But under Chris and Martin's guidance it had dived for more than seven hours, surveying the ship, filming marine life, and peering into the deckhouse. Its small mechanical arm and claw had recovered a trio of artifacts: a round piece of carved wood, a strip of green copper sheeting, and a handsome block from one of the ship's yards.

At first, bringing the artifacts to the surface raised the ire of archaeologist Robert Grenier, a short, heavy-set man in his forties who had been sent to the site by Parks Canada. Grenier's position was a difficult one: surrounded by a gang of highly charged men who had waited three years to dive the *Breadalbane*, he had to ensure that as little as possible was disturbed and that nothing was removed from the ship without his agreement.

Adding to Grenier's difficulty was that he had never worked a deep-water wreck before. His specialty was archaeology in water less than fifteen meters deep. For years he and his associates had been working in the shallow waters of Red Bay, Labrador, on a seventeenth-century Basque ship. No one in Parks Canada knew anything about the impressive performance of the deep-diving systems being used in the Arctic. The first time Robert Grenier had seen a remotely piloted vehicle or an atmospheric diving suit was when he arrived at the campsite.

Long before the 1983 expedition was underway, it had been agreed that anything recovered from the *Breadalbane* would be turned over to Parks Canada. But the wavering question that hung in the air, unexamined, was: what would be done if an opportunity to recover something of real significance presented itself? Who would make the decision? Would it be Grenier? Or would it be a team decision involving Grenier and the operators of the new technology?

"Doug, where the hell are you?"

There was a long pause. Even the roaring of the diesels in the big dive tent seemed to fade. Over the WASP communications set came the sounds of a man grunting. Doug Osborne, a big, muscular man with a thick black moustache hugging his upper lip, looked up through the dome of the WASP suit at the water towering above him. He was on the *Breadalbane*, somewhere on the starboard side. On each of his two earlier dives he had landed on the port side, but this time an eddy in the current had forced him across the deck to the starboard bulwarks. The same current had wrapped his cable around one of the masts. Somewhere in the darkness over his head he was snared by the *Breadalbane*.

At age thirty-four, with more than thirty dives behind him, Osborne was one of the most accomplished WASP pilots in the world. During all of those dives, most of them for the inspection and repair of offshore drilling platforms, he had never felt that his life was at risk. Even now it was not a thought that burdened his mind. Somewhere, off to the port side of the ship, was the RPV with its lights and all-seeing cameras. A second WASP suit was on hand at the surface, ready to dive. With his dive just started, Osborne was still warm. There was plenty of time.

It was basically a problem of relationships, of finding out where the cable lay, above or below the crosstrees, and where and how strong the current was. But there was that nagging doubt: what if the current increased its strength or changed direction? Or the cable was twisted and seized?

He conversed quietly with Nuytten on the intercom. They considered sending the RPV over to see where the cable was snagged, but Nuytten hesitated, concerned lest the two cables become hopelessly snarled if they crossed. A message of caution was sent over to Martin Bowen in the RPV tent, and the remotely piloted vehicle went on its way. On the surface, Nuytten, working mostly with eye contact and hand signals, coordinated the efforts of Terry Thompson, Tom Gilchrest, and Michel Garbay. Using the diesel-driven winch drum, they carefully lowered and lifted the snagged cable, synchronizing their efforts with those of Osborne, deep in the water below them. After a few tense minutes of tight-lining, they pulled him back across the deck the same way he'd gone in.

"O.K. Hold that."

"Roger. All hold . . . where are you?"

"I'm right beside the foremast. My cable's clear. Seems to be resting on a big metal thing, like a windlass or a capstan."

"Roger that. We'll pull you over to the port side and you can go aft."

The RPV came up over Osborne's shoulder splashing its lights into the scene in front of him. With a soft cloth he wiped the dome's glassy surface.

"Negative. Negative. I just want to stay here for a minute." His voice was almost apologetic. "The view is absolutely beautiful. The forward wall of the deckhouse is gone and I'm looking directly into it. Jeez, I can see everything."

And he could. He saw the tables and chairs bathed in bright colours, just as Nuytten had earlier, and he, too, thought of the men who had once occupied the deckhouse, men like himself, talking, laughing, teasing, telling jokes, sharing secrets, in pairs and alone, making plans, reminiscing, confessing fears and uncertainties.

Even to the men glued to the video screens on the surface the colours were riotous. The interior wood-grained walls of the deckhouse were a light tan. Soft coral was everywhere, draped in feathery bunches like vermillion grapes. Osborne stayed for a long time, reluctant to move. Then he backed away and followed the RPV down the port side towards the stern.

As he flew off, just outward from the bulwarks, he glanced down to check the small dials indicating his carbon dioxide and oxygen levels. He reached over to add more oxygen. He had committed to memory Nuytten's instructions for the safest approach to the area behind the deckhouse — "Overfly the stern, turn around, power over the rail" — and he had been there before, but still he had problems with the century-old debris scattered over the stern. After two tries he landed with a soft thump on the thick pine planks of the deck. He could hear his own breathing.

"Say, Doug, we've checked the angle and tension on your cable as it goes through the ice hole. Terry thinks the current is increasing."

Osborne thrust forward and then let the weight of the suit hold him solidly on the deck. Directly in front was the cabinet or box binnacle with the two compasses mounted inside. Below it, covered in coral, was the magnificent shape of the wheel.

He hunched forward, his head and shoulders up in the dome. Most of his last dive had been spent peering into the binnacle, testing it gently with the aluminum tip of one of his manipulators, frustrated by his inability to recover one of the compasses. Both of them were wedged tightly into their shelves, surrounded by hundreds of marble-sized objects that looked like shells. The compasses and the wood that held them were fragile, too fragile to lift without possible damage. After talking to Nuytten he decided to leave them where they were, a decision that pleased the archaeologists.

There were two of them now, Grenier and Charles Arnold, just in from the Prince of Wales Heritage Centre in Yellowknife. For the life of him, Osborne couldn't figure out what all the fuss was about. In the hours before this dive the question of whether or not to recover the wheel had erupted into a controversy, Grenier and the expedition leader locked into their different views of what should be done — one man wanting to leave the wheel untouched, the other wanting Osborne's opinion before making a final decision.

Osborne reached up from inside the suit and scratched the day-old stubble on his chin. The wheel leaned against the wall. It looked free, but its lower half was obscured by soft coral. He straightened out the metallic arm and put the tip of one of the manipulators on the rim. Gently he pushed. The wheel didn't budge. Then he tried to lock the manipulator jaws around the thick wooden rim, but they slipped off. He forced himself lower in the suit and tried to look under the wheel. He would have to get down low enough to get one manipulator, and perhaps both, through the spokes. Slowly he inserted one manipulator and then the other and tried to lock one to another. He could see that the white metal jaws were almost touching. In the process he felt the wheel move. He knew it was free; the trick now was get both metal arms to link up. But he could not close the gap. There was not enough room for him to move.

"O.K., Doug, forget it. We've run out of time. You've been down now an hour and a half."

"But it's loose . . . there's nothing holding it. I just can't get a good grip from this position and I don't want to damage anything."

"Forget it. The current's increasing. Run forward a bit and see if you can find some wood samples and then we'll bring you up."

"Roger that."

Osborne backed out of the hole and started to head forward. He watched as the RPV made its way back to its protective cage thirty meters away. Then he asked for slack in his cable, reversed his thrusters, and went back down towards the wheel.

This time his position was better. Both arms went through, the left one over the king spoke.

On the surface there was silence. The winch drum holding the cable unwound until it came to a piece of grey tape marking the position of the diver on the stern.

"Doug. Where the hell are you?"

There was a long pause, broken by the sounds of a man wrestling with something.

Osborne, his heart slamming against his chest, pushed hard enough to lock the two jaws together.

"I've got it — I've got the sucker. Stand by to take up slack. I can lift it. I've got a good grip on it." The he closed his eyes. On the surface, Nuytten pressed his palms together.

"O.K., buddy, here we go. Taking up your slack."

Osborne had committed himself. Holding onto the wheel with both arms, he could barely work the thrusters. He would ride up past the debris and the deckhouse at the whim of the current and the tension in his cable. He would ride up betrothed to a great uncertainty about the metal arms. They were held on by pressure. They were not built for lifting. If the weight of the wheel was too much and they tore off, the ocean would fill the suit in seconds.

And so Osborne rode up towards the ice, he and the suit and the wheel, balanced on that keen edge of endeavour that suggests that somehow, human capacity is what it has to be.

Three days later the campsite was clear except for some man-banked snow, a few pieces of plywood, and dark rectangles of thin ice where the two dive holes had been. All the tons of equipment, and the men who had operated it, were back at the base camp in Resolute. My son Jeff and I were the last ones to leave, and with the Twin Otter warming up in the background we made a final inspection. Here was where the kitchen and the RPV tent used to be; there was where Osborne had returned to the ice; there was where Grenier, a big smile on his face, had accepted the wheel. In the far corner of the dive hole was a small, round opening surrounded by fresh prints on the snow. It was the work of a ring seal, a reminder that in a few days, after the next snowfall, there would be no evidence of our being here.

EPILOGUE

October, 1984. Jeff and I were together at a campsite on the French River in Ontario. As the last of the embers went out, we gazed across the dark surface of the river that had carried so many *voyageurs* and explorers westward. Leaning forward to poke the fire, Jeff asked me if I had seen the recent colour photographs of John Torrington, one of Franklin's men whose frozen body had been exhumed after lying for one hundred and thirty-eight years in the permafrost of Beechey Island. The pictures showed him to be fully dressed in shirt and trousers, almost as if he'd just fallen asleep. As we talked about Torrington and the strange sensations we had felt as we stood over his grave that summer in 1975, I began to wonder what he and his band of brave men would have thought of our eight-year endeavour: the months in the archives, the years of search, the discovery, and, finally, the dives to the *Breadalbane*. I suspect that they would probably have been intrigued by the technology, fascinated by what had been done by men not much different from themselves. Perhaps they would have smiled at the fact that, as yet, no one has been able to locate Sir John Franklin or his two ships, *Erebus* and *Terror*. But they would have liked knowing that after more than a century — they have not been forgotten.

SOME HISTORICAL HIGHLIGHTS OF THE EXPLORATION OF THE NORTHWEST PASSAGE

1576	Frobisher's first voyage in search of the Northwest Passage.
1585 - 1587	Davis searches the shores of Labrador and Baffin Island for the Passage.
1610	Hudson sails into Hudson Bay and is abandoned there by his crew.
1616	Bylot and Baffin sail into the northern reaches of Baffin Bay.
1818	Ross sails as far as Lancaster Sound but turns back at its entrance.
1819 - 1820	Parry makes his classic voyage into Lancaster Sound — over 800 km — and spends the winter at Melville Island.
1819 - 1820	Franklin's first expedition to the arctic coast via the Coppermine River.
1825 - 1827	Franklin's second expedition to the arctic coast via the MacKenzie River.
1829 - 1833	Ross sails into the central Arctic.
1845 - 1848	Franklin's ill-fated voyage in *Erebus* and *Terror*.
1848	Plans made to rescue Franklin — Sir James Ross fails to find any traces.
1848 - 1850	Many expeditions — overland and by sea — including those of Austin, Richardson, Pullen, M'Clure and Collinsen, fail to find Franklin or his ships.
1852	Belcher sails with five ships including the *North Star* to search the central Arctic for Franklin. *North Star* is anchored off Beechey Island.
1850 - 1854	M'Clure's ship wrecked — survivors walk to Beechey Island and are the first men to cross the Northwest Passage.

189

1853	The *Breadalbane* sinks off Beechey Island.
1854	Rae finds traces of the Franklin expedition.
1857 - 1859	M'Clintock finds more traces of the Franklin expedition.
1903 - 1906	Amundsen's *Gjoa* is the first ship to sail through the Northwest Passage.

FURTHER READING

The Exploration of Northern Canada
Alan Cooke and Clive Holland
The Arctic History Press - 1978

The Discovery of The Northwest Passage
Capt. R. M'Clure 1850-1854
M.G. Hurtig Ltd. (Reprinted 1969)

Frozen Ships — The Arctic Diary of Johann Miertsching 1850 - 1854
Translated by L.H. Neatby
Macmillan 1967

The Way of a Ship
Alan Villiers
Charles Scribner's Sons 1970

The Rise and Fall of British Naval Mastery
Paul M. Kennedy
Allen Wane - Penguin Books 1976

Search For Franklin
Leslie H. Neatby
M.G. Hurtig Ltd. 1970

Arctic Breakthrough
Paul Nanton
Clarke Irwin 1970, 1981

The Hot Arctic
John Dyson
Little Brown and Co. 1979